LAUGHTER, THE BEST MEDICINE

By the same author:

Stress Busters
Living Wonderfully

LAUGHTER,
THE BEST MEDICINE

The Healing Powers of
Happiness, Humour and Joy!

Robert Holden

Thorsons
An Imprint of HarperCollinsPublishers

Thorsons
An Imprint of HarperCollins*Publishers*
77–85 Fulham Palace Road,
Hammersmith, London W6 8JB

Published by Thorsons 1993
7 9 10 8 6

© Robert Holden 1993

Robert Holden asserts the moral right to be
identified as the author of this work

A catalogue record for this book
is available from the British Library

ISBN 0 7225 2827 2

Printed in Great Britain by
Clays Ltd, St Ives plc

To Avanti Kumar and to Philip Churm –
your friendships are inspirational!
Thank you, both of you, for being who you are.

CONTENTS

Acknowledgements   9

Introduction   11

1   Releasing the Fun Child Within   15

2   Laughter, the Best Medicine   33

3   Humour, Happiness and Health   55

4   Laughter and Society   76

5   'Smile Management' at Work   98

6   The Art of Living Joyfully   115

Directory of Humour Resources   131

ACKNOWLEDGEMENTS

Thank you to the West Birmingham Health Authority (WBHA) for your courage, vision and support. In March 1989, the WBHA encouraged me to set up the first free NHS Stress Buster Clinic in Great Britain, and in September 1991 they allowed me to set up the first free NHS Laughter Clinic in Great Britain.

Researching this book has been a lot of laughs – I did not imagine in the beginning that there could be so much fun in medicine, and so much medicine in fun! I would like to acknowledge the work of all the people around the world who are pioneers in this most joyful of subjects. I also want to thank two psychology students, Marie Paine and Polly Phillipson – together we have helped one another along the way to our own individual goals.

I want to acknowledge the people in the world who, each in his or her individual way, encourage me to laugh, to love and to live. Thank you, especially, to Sally Holden, my lovely mum, and David Holden, my 'favourite' (and only) brother. Thank you to my fiancée, Miranda who, when I asked her to marry me, laughed uproariously (honked and guffawed more like) for two solid minutes before she said 'yes' – I know it was two minutes because it felt like fifteen! Thank you to my inspirational grandmother, Dorothy Hill. And thank you to my fantastic friends, Avanti Kumar, Philip Churm, Raina Kumar, Lilla Bek, Robert Redfern and Michael Furber. Lastly, a very big thank you to Erica Smith and to Judith Kendra, my two editors, and to Barbara Vesey, who have helped me to realize my vision of *Laughter, the Best Medicine*.

INTRODUCTION:
WELCOME TO THE
LAUGHTER CLINIC

How would you feel if on visiting your doctor with a problem, he or she gave you a personal prescription not for pills but to attend a workshop on how to enjoy yourself more?!

A burst of happy, spontaneous laughter is one of the most delightful, wholesome and highly prized of all human experiences. Instinctively we each of us know that laughing can help us feel healthy, alive and well again. Moments of laughter are moments to savour, for each time we laugh we are fortified, uplifted and nourished. Have you ever met anyone who does not agree with the ancient affirmation, 'Laughter is the best medicine'?

It may surprise you to know that modern Western medicine is, in certain quarters, totally tickled with the idea of 'laughter medicine'. Since the 1950s, in particular, well over 500 medical research papers have been published on the potential medicinal worth of mirth. Serious-minded psychologists have presented over 1,000 papers on the same subject since the 1940s. It would appear that the modern schools of medical science and psychology are at last catching up with the ancient schools of common sense!

Laughter medicine is not a new phenomenon. The healing properties of laughter, happiness and joy are acknowledged many times in the holy books of Christianity, Judaism, Hinduism, Islam, Sikhism and Taoism, and also in Buddhism's legend of the Laughing Buddha. Anthropologists have unearthed evidence of laughter medicine in the most ancient cultures. For example, one South American rainforest community held a festival of laughter and happiness whenever one of its people fell seriously ill, so as to speed healing and recovery.

In northeast Asia, the first duty of the doctor of ancient times was to encourage patients to 'laugh into the face of misfortune'. The medicine men of the old African tribes would, in an attempt to drive out the morbid demons of malady and distemper, wear the costume of clown, dancer or entertainer. And in ancient Greece, amphitheatres were often sited next to the healing temples so that patients could enjoy comedy and entertainment as part of their convalescence. 'The best of healers is good cheer,' wrote Pindar, the Greek poet of the fifth century BC.

The recent renewed interest in laughter medicine has coincided with the modern resurrection of humanistic and holistic models of health care, which recognize that as well as physical, chemical and biological causes of *dis-ease* there are also emotional, mental, social and spiritual ones. Laughter, as a possible therapeutic tool, is once again a serious proposition as health professionals become increasingly aware that health, wholeness, humour and happiness are interrelated.

My model of medicine is inspired by personal beliefs and medical research that affirm that, in order to be healthy, it helps to be happy. Health is a means to an end – it is a passport to a full, free-flowing form of living and unfoldment. I describe health as a *vibrant, dynamic and harmonious interplay between body–mind–soul* and also between

Self–Society–Life. Absence of illness is not health; true health is joy!

Under the auspices of the West Birmingham Health Authority, my NHS Laughter Clinic offers creative time and space to explore some of the most important, valuable issues of life. At the Laughter Clinic we express ourselves, we explore ourselves and we play some of the most important *creative growth games* I know of. Regular themes include the pursuit of happiness, the art of joyful living, happy thinking, the inner smile, releasing the fun child, personal enjoyment and fulfilment, the therapeutic power of play, happy relationships and making 'fun time'.

Love, laughter and living are three great prizes in life. At the Laughter Clinic we recognize that laughter is as much a basic need as are love and the courage to live. Thus we aim to *en*courage and to empower one another to open up to life through love and laughter. Life, the great tragi-comedy, will continue to send us burdens, but there will be blessings, too. The better we live with the blessings, the better we will live with the burdens also.

Body and mind share an ecology that must work in harmony in order to provide health. Order is the key. 'In a disordered mind, as in a disordered body, soundness of health is impossible,' wrote the Roman philosopher Cicero. The holistic models of health have quite clearly identified that feelings of fear, self-doubt, anxiety, powerlessness, hopelessness and depression are as potentially physically harmful as are bacterias, germs, viruses and infections.

If negative thoughts, feelings and emotions can hold up health, what then can positive thoughts, feelings and emotions achieve? Could it be that an ability to laugh, the courage to smile, a propensity for hope and optimism, a readiness to radiate good humour and a playful disposition are healthful frames of mind that may accelerate healing and recovery from illness? What role, if any, can the patient play in his or her own practical recovery?

The energizing effects of laughter are often reproduced, with slight variations, in happy, positive feelings and emotions such as hope, joy, happiness, optimism and the will to live. These feelings and emotions are the vital catalysts that recreate, reactive and re-empower the human spirit. These 'energies' are a form of self-prescribed medicine that has measurable physical, emotional, mental and spiritual effects. Like laughter, they can light up body, mind and soul.

The success of the NHS Laughter Clinic has been meteoric. It grows, day by day, in response to a social crisis and illness that I can only describe as a *dearth of happiness*. Happiness is fast becoming a lost art. We are in danger of forgetting how to be truly happy within ourselves and also with each other. Laughter, like love, is an important key to the happiness, growth and healing of us all.

Be brave, be daring! Find your happiness; do not fear it. Then, share your happiness with everyone, and your joy will expand and exceed your greatest imaginings.

Happy reading. Happy living!

Robert Holden
The Laughter Clinic
June 1993

1

RELEASING THE
FUN CHILD WITHIN

*The heart which is not struck by the sweet smiles of an
infant is still asleep.*
Hazrat Inayat Khan

Is there anything quite so heart-warming as the smile of an
infant? Such inspiration! A mere memory of a child's smile,
or even imagining one, can stir such vivid, soul-deep feelings
of hope, love, delight and laughter. Such joy! We are young
again. We are awake again; aware again; alive again. A small
flame deep within us is rekindled and begins to glow; and
when we look into the light we find there our own *inner fun
child*, at play.

Smiling is an innate human expression. Deaf children
smile. Blind children smile. All children of all cultures smile.
The first smile tends to shine anytime within the first six
weeks of life. Once discovered, a child will play with smiles
all day long, particularly if he or she is encouraged to do so.
Indeed, a child quickly finds that smiling is friendly, fun and
something that all humans like to respond to.

Smiling is a child's first language. Shared smiles offer a way
of communicating, interacting and relating. A child soon
learns, for instance, that smiling gains attention, communicates needs and facilitates understanding. A child's
smile speaks to us in so many ways and on so many levels.
Above all, perhaps, it can touch and rekindle that aspect of
us that is also unique, innocent and wonder-full.

Where do smiles come from? How are they born? How do they grow? Psychologists agree to disagree! Behavioural psychologists tend to believe that a child's smile begins life as one of many insignificant random muscular facial movements. The very first smile is, therefore, almost an accident, but because it gets such a positive, joyous response from mum, or whoever is around at the time, the child performs an encore! The bigger and better the encore, the bigger and better the response, and so on. Smiling is therefore a product of positive reinforcement.

Some psychologists believe that the physical action of smiling first evolves from the physical action of crying. Similarly, Gestalt psychologists often assert that smiling develops as a natural counterpart to crying. Smiling evokes comfort and care. Another theory suggests that smiling develops from the muscular movements of the lips and mouth during feeding. Therefore, a child likes to smile because smiling imitates the pleasurable movements made during times of physical nourishment and sustenance.

Yet another theory describes smiling as a physical reflex that responds in particular to tickling. A child smiles when touched in the most ticklish areas of his or her body, which are those parts with protective reflexes such as the armpits, the ribs, the soles of the feet, around the neck and under the chin. Similarly, some psychoanalysts believe smiling stems from a 'pleasure reflex' or 'pleasure response' to stroking of the lips, cheeks and chin.

The 'wind theory' is perhaps the most disconcerting of all smile theories for parents because it suggests that smiling first evolves from the effort, pleasure and process of 'bottom-snorting'! Initially, then, a child's smile is a product of posterior pursuits. However, when a child recognizes that adults respond well to the smile, then he or she will smile more often.

Most smile theories acknowledge that smiling is initially a physical behaviour that evolves into an emotional, mental and even spiritual one. There are a few theories, however, that maintain that smiling and laughter are *essentially* soulful, spiritual actions. Whatever the theory, the smile of a child, once established, plays a vital, nurturing role that helps to inspire and to support close, happy, playful and loving relationships.

Laughter takes a little longer than smiling. The first observable signs of laughter tend to happen any time between week four and week ten of life. It is generally acknowledged that a child's experience of laughter becomes well established by about the fourth month. Some theories state that laughter evolves from smiling; other theories claim that laughter and smiling are two separate behaviours. Once again, whatever the theory, laughter plays a similar role to smiling in helping to create and to sustain positive, joyful, life-affirming relationships.

LOVE AND LAUGHTER

Love sees as a child sees.
Anonymous

Each and every child is born with what I call a *superabundant creative potential* for laughter, fun, play, happiness and love. It is part of the natural 'unconditioning' of a child to look for laughter, to create fun, to indulge in play, to spread happiness and to radiate and receive love. By contrast, fear, anger, hatred, depression and anxiety, for instance, are not natural; they are learned, particularly in later life when the adult in us takes over from the child.

This superabundant creative potential never dies. We carry it with us throughout adolescence, adulthood and old age; it remains alive and kicking for as long as we do. The one danger, however, is that the light of our inner child can easily become eclipsed and forgotten if we allow ourselves to trudge tiredly, tediously and unthinkingly into the unnatural conditioning of adulthood. To hold on to our inner fun child we must stay awake, we must stay alive – *fully alive*.

A newborn child invokes so many powerful feelings in an adult: joy, happiness, love and a profound sense of personal peace with the world. This peacefulness feels a million light years away from the adult 'games' of occupational stress, personal conflict, divorce, mid-life crisis and executive burnout. To travel into adulthood alone, with our inner child 'not seen and not heard', deprives us of maturity, fulfilment and a certain inner contentedness.

To see life through the eyes of a child, our own inner child, lends a strength of peace and harmony to adulthood. Dr Gerald Jampolsky in his delightful article 'Children as Teachers of Peace' encourages us all to reclaim our inner child. He writes, 'If we can see life as children do, with their clarity and simplicity of thought, their trust, and their innate capacity for joy and laughter, we can find very practical solutions to every problem we face.'

The newborn child wants to belong, to bond and to be at one with his or her fellow human playmates. Laughter connects us – both inside and out. Through laughter, fun and play a child expresses his or her deepest natural urges, which are to be at peace and at one with all life. We are none of us ever too old to re-experience and reclaim these natural birthrights.

Isolation, separation and unnatural divisions between people create a split not only in the communities of society but also in the community of the Self. Our inner child holds the keys for health, harmony and happiness. As Bertrand Russell once wrote in *The Conquest of Happiness*, 'To be happy in this world, especially when youth is past, it is necessary to feel oneself not merely an isolated individual whose day will soon be over, but part of the stream of life flowing on from the first germ to the remote and unknown future.'

PLAY

We do not stop playing because we are old; we grow old because we stop playing.

Anonymous

As children, our days were filled with play. Our appetite for play appeared to be perpetual; few adults could go the distance! The best times were playtimes. Play built us up physically. Through play, we learned to explore, to experience and to express ourselves. Playtime was a time for laughter, fun, happiness and creativity. We experienced friendship, sharing and co-operation. Play was also a wonderful time for developing skills, talents, confidence and self-esteem. Why, therefore, do so many adults feel they must abandon play?

Play is the ideal preparation for life. As a child, play is at once both frivolously fun and profoundly serious. Early childhood is an adventure of discovery. Play is a form of learning. The child who does not play, therefore, or who is not allowed to play, runs the risk of a serious setback in life. This setback will manifest itself physically, emotionally, mentally and spiritually. This is equally true for adults.

While an adult will often only play to kill time or to rest a while, a child is constantly on the look-out for opportunities to play and to be creative. Dorothy Einon, a psychologist who studies play, writes in her book *Creative Play*, 'Almost everything a child does – when not asked to do something else – is play. It can be solitary, social, idle or energetic; it is frequently (to the adult) boring and repetitive; but it is almost always creative in some sense.' Children live to play.

Psychologists have identified the many different stages of play that appear from age 2 to 5. Almost from the start, children like to indulge in *solitary play*. The next development is sometimes called *parallel play*, in which two children play in close proximity but apart. Then comes *associative play*, in which children will play together but without rules, co-ordination or organization. *Co-operative play*, or *social play*, describes a pattern of play where children share, co-operate and interact more fully with one another. As each month passes, a child's play will become increasingly more frequent, complex, imaginative, creative and social.

A part of the fun of play is skill development. There are four main sets of skills children discover and develop through play. The first set of skills is confidence skills, which can include, for instance, learning about purpose, direction, success and achievement. Through play a child also learns about imagination, music, art, dance and movement. These are creativity skills. Relationship skills are gained next. These teach a child about camaraderie, sharing, helpfulness, team work and compromise. And then there are the life skills that play provides, such as perception training, cognitive development, the importance of perseverance and other similar lessons.

No one is ever too old to play. Indeed, the spirit of play lives forever within us in our inner fun child. Not all adults give up their play. On the contrary, some develop their play as they would any other talent or skill. Through our day-to-day existence we all have the chance to play out roles, emotions, wishes, challenges, ambitions and many other experiences. Life is often described as a classroom; it is also a playground. The spirit of play can be our greatest resource for inspiration, energy, creativity, self-realization, development and growth.

Play can also be a therapy, a medicine and a natural healer that promotes humour, happiness and wholeness. An absence of fun, little or no playtime and a lack of laughter are common symptoms of stress, sickness and *dis-ease*. Little or no time for play can also be a significant cause of illness and disharmony. On the other hand, frequent prescriptions of play can inspire rest, relaxation and recovery. Play is also an act of 're-creation'. Through play we can recharge, revitalize and re-energize ourselves back into life.

To be able to play for the sake of play, with no thought of reward, victory or defeat, is perhaps the highest form of fun. When the participation means more than the result, play can become an evolutionary experience that lends expression to the fullness of Self. Play becomes an adventure in which we indulge ourselves, accept ourselves and give of ourselves, all at once. It was Ovid who wrote in *The Art of Love*, 'In our play we reveal what kind of people we are.' Play can also sometimes give us the courage to be who we want to be. Play is our liberation.

FUN

Life was a funny thing that occurred on the way to the grave.
Quentin Crisp

Children have a fervent fascination for fun. Give children any task or any object, even a loo roll, and they can, if they wish, find some fun in it. By contrast many adults suffer from 'fun-droughts', the 'boredom-bug', over-seriousness, depression and other forms of spiritual malnourishment. They mislay, forget or neglect to tend their natural love of fun. If you're wise you will never overlook the fruitful importance of fun in your life. Run without fun and your stride will falter.

To allow a spirit of fun to carry you along in life is indeed the mark of creative genius. To invest a sense of fun into everything you do fires your creative imagination. Give a child an ordinary wooden spoon and it soon becomes a rocket, cricket bat, portable phone, magic wand, trumpet or drum stick. Children's innate, imaginative genius develops best through fun, play and laughter.

Adult geniuses such as Albert Einstein or Thomas Edison invested huge amounts of fun into their work. It was a spirit of fun and adventure that fuelled their enthusiasm. Norman Vincent Peale addresses this point in his edited treasury of *Joy and Enthusiasm*: 'What is the outstanding characteristic of a small child?' he writes, 'It is enthusiasm! He thinks the world is terrific; he loves it; everything fascinates him . . . Too few persons retain this excitement, and a reason is that they let enthusiasm be drained off. If you are not getting as much from life as you want, examine the state of your enthusiasm.'

The fun child within us is an entrepreneur, an explorer and an adventurer. Our instinctive capacity for fun feeds our curiosity, our creative conjecture and contemplation. Diane Arbus captured marvellously the spirit of the fun child when she wrote, 'My favourite thing is to go where I've never been.' Each and every day is a new life, a fresh beginning and an unexplored opportunity for the fun child in us; by contrast, the adult in us believes he or she has seen it all before. Each and every day it is good to let your fun child wander through a world that is, truly, wonder-full.

Fun also supports 'flow'. The spontaneous, all-embracing nature of fun can allow us to lose ourselves in what we are doing. Sportspeople often talk of 'peak experience' in which everything they do flows perfectly, almost as if they were being guided by a higher self. Dr Mihaly Csikszentmihalyi has studied the relationship between fun and flow. In his book *Flow: The Psychology of Optimal Experience*, he describes how human intensity, enthusiasm and total immersion in a task or project leads to a feeling of flow, or overdrive, in which object and subject, space and time, meet with one another. The results are almost always joyful.

Certain exercises and disciplines have been found to facilitate this sense of flow, such as meditation, breath and relaxation techniques, T'ai Chi, martial arts, creative drawing, dance and yoga. Dr Csikszentmihalyi believes fun and flow can be found in any activity, from hang-gliding to hoovering. His observations are inspired by a world-wide tradition of wisdom and philosophy that encourages the actor to allow himself or herself to become one with the action. Fun is the key, flow is the experience, and freedom is the result. A good sense of fun can, truly, set us free.

SILLINESS

Being silly is not silly; being silly is a first step to being free.
R. Holden

The word *silly* is derived from two old European words: *seely* and *saelig*, both of which mean 'blessed', 'happy' and 'joyful'. Irrational, odd and bizarre silliness tends to send a child dizzy with delight. Children enjoy being really silly; adults rarely understand. Silliness offers a natural, easy source of happiness and merriment to children. To be silly also serves some very serious functions in early life. A child needs silliness for healthy, creative mental and emotional growth; so too, actually, do adults!

Children are natural comedians. They love to look for, identify and play with endless possibilities of nonsense, absurdity and silliness. One of the most important functions of silliness is that the act of being silly helps to keep the mind young, fresh, alive and relatively unconditioned. The less silly a person is the more conditioned he or she becomes. Silliness allows the mind to breathe easy and to be free from the cobwebs and constraints of conformity, seriousness and dull, adult conditioning and limitation. 'A little rebellion now and then is a good thing,' wrote Thomas Jefferson.

Silliness often inspires creativity, original thought,

invention and innovation. How many times have you heard a really good idea introduced as, 'I know this might seem really silly, but . . .'? Indeed, as the English mathematician and philosopher Alfred North Whitehead once wrote, 'The "silly" question is the first intimation of some totally new development.' Copernicus, the Polish astronomer, was at first considered silly for stating that the sun, not the earth, was the centre of the solar system; Alexander Graham Bell's idea of a telephone sounded initially very silly; and as for travel to the moon!

Being silly often proves a point. Silliness can inspire wisdom and philosophy. The fool, the clown or the court jester of medieval times was employed not only for his juggling skills, but also for his judgement, perception and inventive thought. Wit and wisdom went hand in hand. Silliness can suggest a new angle, a fresh perspective, lateral thinking and novel ideas. A truly great thinker will always take the time to entertain the 'silly factor', for there is always some buried treasure to be found by doing so.

Silliness also serves to calm, pacify and control the ego. 'You grow up the day you have the first real laugh – at yourself,' wrote Ethel Barrymore. The ability to laugh at yourself is one more serious, vital function of silliness. All in all, then, for an adult to ignore the importance of silliness can be very sad, very dangerous and, above all, truly silly!

RELEASING YOUR FUN CHILD

When I grow up I want to be a little boy.
Joseph Heller, *Something Happened*

As I said earlier, each of us carries within ourselves a fun child. The fun child describes that aspect of you which is, now and forever, unique, new, original and innocent. It is that part of you that believes that you (and everyone else) have a right to be happy, to be joyful and, above all, to celebrate life and living. The fun child is a fundamental feature of our physical, mental, emotional and spiritual anatomy – we cannot grow up properly without it.

And this fun child wants to play! The fun child is essentially a creative spirit that manifests itself best through invention, laughter, play and art. Poets, writers and artists tend traditionally to have a well-developed awareness and appreciation of their inner child. To see the world through the eyes of a child can inspire artistic genius. Much of what an artist does is to recapture the intensity, the vitality and the 'for-the-first-time' feeling of childhood. The child is no less than the adult; often the child is teacher to the adult. It was the poet William Wordsworth who wrote, 'The child is father of the man.'

The great spiritual traditions of our world pay homage to the child. 'Blessed be childhood,' wrote Henri Frederic Amiel, 'for it brings down something of heaven into the midst of our rough earthliness.' Jesus described God as 'Father', and addressed us as 'Children', not in some derogatory sense but rather to remind us of our original nature. The child is a symbol of our highest Self. 'One laugh of a child will make the holiest day more sacred still,' wrote Robert G. Ingersoll.

In the Eastern spiritual traditions the inner child is referred to many times and in many ways. The Taoist tradition, for instance, makes reference to 'the uncarved block' which is that part of us that is unconditioned, unsoiled and untouched. The aim of the adept is to become one again with this uncarved block. Similarly, in Hindu philosophy much mention is made of the Cosmic Egg, which also describes our original nature.

Modern psychology recognizes the importance of the continuing role of the inner child in adult life. Eric Berne, father of Transactional Analysis, identified three main ego states, or patterns of feeling, thinking and behaviour: 'parent', 'adult' and 'child'. In other words, we deal with some people and situations as if we were parents, some as adults, and others as if we were children.

Eric Berne considered what he called the 'natural child' to be in many ways the most essential of all ego states in that it inspires spontaneous, creative, original and natural behaviour. Failure to express the natural child creates problems for the adult and parent within us. These problems manifest themselves in the 'games' we play, particularly in our relationships with others. Most of these games are unhealthy, manipulative, 'win-lose' games as opposed to healthy, generous and genuinely 'win-win' games.

An essential challenge of life, therefore, is to nurture and care consciously for the spiritual fun child within. A sombre adult or a highly critical parent, for instance, can be enough to silence the child. The key is to integrate the inner parent, adult and child so as to create a whole family and a whole Self. The child has equal status. He or she can vote at any age!

To keep yourself fresh and young it is essential that you take time to play with your own inner fun child. At the Laughter Clinic we aim to give the fun child full rein. Alexander Chase once wrote, 'There are few successful adults who were not first successful children.' The same can be said for happy adults and happy children. The real aim is not to grow out of the child, but rather to grow up *with* the child.

CREATIVE GROWTH GAMES

THE 'NEWNESS OF LIFE' GAME

The Indian poet Rabindranath Tagore beseeched, 'Please do not say, "It is morning," and dismiss it with a name of yesterday. See it for the first time as a newborn child that has no name.' Each day is a new day that has never happened before. Young children live in the moment: their senses of sight, hearing, touch, taste and smell are all finely attuned to the new, the novel and the *now*.

Each and every day we are born anew, if we allow ourselves to be. Today is both the first time and the last time. Ask yourself 'What can I look for, listen to, think about and do that is new, today?' Apply these questions each and every day to your work, your journeys and your relationships so that you keep fresh, open and, above all, thankful. Each day, by way of celebrating you are alive, challenge yourself, as a child would, to experience something new. Make today a new beginning.

THE 'LIFE AS LEARNING' GAME

Learning is a life-long experience. All the world is a school; all the world is a playground, too. It was Henry Ford, the great innovator of the automobile, who wrote, 'Anyone who stops learning is old, whether at 20 or 80. Anyone who keeps learning stays young. The greatest thing in life is to keep your mind young.' There is always something new to learn. The fun child makes learning fun!

Robert Fulghum's book *All I Really Need to Know I Learned in Kindergarten* has become essential reading at the Laughter Clinic. In it he writes:

All I really need to know about how to live and what to do and how to be I learned in kindergarten. Wisdom was not at the top of the graduate-school mountain, but there in the sandpile at Sunday School. These are the things I learned:

Share everything.
Play fair.
Don't hit people.

Put things back where you found them.

Clean up your own mess.

Don't take things that aren't yours.

Say you're sorry when you hurt somebody.

Wash your hands before you eat.

Flush.

Warm cookies and cold milk are good for you.

Live a balanced life – learn some and think some and draw and paint and sing and dance and play and work every day some.

Take a nap every afternoon.

When you go out into the world, watch out for traffic, hold hands, and stick together.

Be aware of wonder. Remember the little seed in the Styrofoam cup: The roots go down and the plant goes up and nobody really knows how or why, but we are all like that.

Goldfish and hamsters and white mice and even the little seed in the Styrofoam cup – they all die. So do we.

And then remember the Dick-and-Jane books and the first word you learned – the biggest word of all – LOOK.

What have you and your fun child learned today?

THE 'PLAYTIME' GAME

Know the value of playtime. Each and every day of your life set aside a little time (or a lot) for play. Allow the spirit of play to be present in all that you do. Play with the concept that every time you go out to work, you are really going out to play. Anytime can be playtime; anything can be play-full. One of the saddest sights you will see in life is an adult who has forgotten how to play. Make sure you do not become a sad sight.

So much of what we treasure, value and aspire to can be achieved through play, such as laughter, friendship, fun, creativity, relaxation, freedom from worry, union, joy and shared experience. It is really true that we spend too much time as 'human doings' and not enough as human beings. Hold on to your interests, your hobbies, your creative talents and your playtime pursuits – you must not allow these things to drown in the economic seas of our 'over-material, cost-effective world'. Nurture, every day, your sense of fun and play.

THE 'BE BIZARRE' GAME

Play is best described as the 'exultation of all that is possible'. Our imaginations open us up to a world of all possibilities. To live imaginatively, aware of the magic in the world, allows us to see these hidden possibilities. In order to live life this creatively and this fully you must be prepared to entertain the ridiculous, the nonsensical and the silly from time to time.

When was the last time you did something really bizarre? When was the last time you showed off your eccentric side? Do not allow the adult in you to dismiss these questions before your fun child has had time to answer. Set yourself a goal to do something bizarre, silly and/or eccentric at least once a week. Take a cue from Lewis Carroll's *Alice in Wonderland* and send someone a 'Happy *Un*birthday' card; devise a crazy calling card or a novel answerphone message; create an 'eccentrics' night out' among friends or colleagues. Do your duty: don your Super-Humour-Person cape and save the world from the arch villain Over-Seriousness!

THE 'WONDER-FULL' GAME

A newborn child exudes energy, vitality and spirit. By contrast, the average adult lopes along in life mostly in neutral gear. He or she is free-wheeling, taking it mostly for granted and has apparently 'seen it all before'. To keep happy, you must keep cultivating wonder.

Dr Gerald Jampolsky in his article 'Children as Teachers of Peace' writes,

> *At the time of this writing, I am 57 years old, and I am doing my best to devote all my energies to unlearning the so-called 'realities' of the world I have accepted. I am attempting to learn that there is an innocent child within me and everyone else, and that the infant's reality is the only true reality.*
>
> *. . . We must keep reminding ourselves that our children are our true mirrors. Let us keep the sparkle in our eyes ignited, and the effervescence of laughter continuous and everlasting in our hearts. Let us make each instant one in which there is a newborn celebration of love.*

One way to celebrate with wonder is to develop an appetite for saying 'thank you'. Make a list of at least 100 things you can be thankful for and spend a moment in grateful prayer and contemplation for each of these 100 'gifts'. If 100 thank-yous is too easy, stretch yourself to 200! If you need a clue or two, think of all the things you would miss terribly if they were suddenly to vanish – i.e., the ability to walk, see or taste; the blue sky, a favourite composition or your close companions. To live best, be blessed!

THE 'CHILD-LIKE' GAME

Have you ever tried to step inside the mind of a child? A young mind has an energy and intensity that fuels imagination, creativity and original, innovative thought. It is a mark of genius to hold on to a 'child-like' attitude to life. Aldous Huxley explains, 'A child-like man is not a man whose development has been arrested; on the contrary, he is a man who has given himself a chance of continuing to develop long after most adults have muffled themselves in the cocoon of middle-aged habit and convention.'

Make a conscious effort to see the world through the eyes of a child. Be a 'Why-s Guy': keep questioning, keep curious and keep contemplating. Be aware; be awake; be alive. Keep curious.

THE 'CHILDHOOD REVISITED' GAME

What are your most vivid, joyful memories of childhood? What were your happiest moments? It is good to revisit childhood and to share childhood memories. Adults are often too quick to consign their childhood to the forgotten file. With some adults it is hard to believe they ever *were* children. Maybe this was this the point Groucho Marx was trying to make when he quipped, 'My mother loved children – she would have given anything if I'd have been one.'

When in the presence of a child who is joyful, playsome and happy, often the problems of our lives seem to fall into perspective. We make contact with our own fun child and we too find permission again to play, to think originally, to laugh, to have fun, to feel freely and to revisit the happiest times of our own child-days.

CO-OPERATIVE GAMES

Co-operative Games, or New Games, are names given to a modern movement that promotes creative, non-competitive play. One exponent of these games is Mildren Masheder who, in her book *Let's Play Together* writes, 'We all, young and old, have a child inside us who needs to be acknowledged and played with; it is part of our intuitive and spontaneous nature and, by nurturing it, we can become more complete and fulfilled.'

Joel Goodman, founder of the Humor Project, is also a pioneer of the Co-operative Games movement. He runs workshops, or Playfairs, across the world in an aim to remind people how to play for fun again. Dale LeFevre is well known for his innovative work with New Games. He explains, 'My focus has gone from rediscovering playfulness to finding that the spirit of play is an invaluable part of my total spirit. It's a way to make contact with my true being. My life is becoming a game of spiritual discovery.' (See the Directory of Humour Resources – page 131).

2

LAUGHTER, THE BEST MEDICINE

Imagine the following scene: three mothers, one father, two young girls and two young boys occupy a small waiting room at a children's hospital. Apart from a wall full of cartoons, a tray of clown masks with a written invitation to 'Please Take Me' and an imaginative arrangement of toys in one corner of the room, the waiting room is otherwise quite 'normal'.

It does not take long to notice that the room is filled with a thick, almost tangible air of tension, fear and apprehension. The parents sit quietly – stiff, upright and tense, avoiding eye-contact. One mother holds a tissue close to her face, occasionally wiping her eyes. Although you suspect she may be crying, you cannot be quite sure. The tension is particularly acute because all four parents have bought their children to visit a specialist. Their children suffer from leukaemia; they await chemotherapy.

At two minutes to eleven o'clock the sound of approaching footsteps is heard. The parents anticipate they are about to meet the specialist; the children stop playing and look up towards the door. Nobody breathes. The door opens and three men in white coats enter.

These 'doctors' look strangely disturbed: one carries a six-foot wobbly syringe and makes duck sounds; another carries a stethoscope which leaks an abundance of soapy bubbles; and the other, with a head of blue and orange hair, pours a top-class cup of tea for each of the parents.

Now the parents are talking with one another; they are, all

of them, bemused and amused. The children are in ecstasy.
'Where is the specialist?' asks one of the mothers. 'Oh, she
always arrives at a quarter past the hour for her eleven o'clock
clinic,' replies one of the clowns (who is, by the way, a fully-
trained counsellor). 'What is all this, then?' asks another
parent. 'This,' replies one of the clowns, 'is laughter
medicine.'

'INTERNAL MASSAGE'

*O, glorious laughter! Thou man-loving spirit, that for a
time doth take the burden from the weary back.*

Douglas Jerrold

'Doctor of Humour' William Fry Jr, MD, has dedicated over
30 years to researching the potential therapeutic properties
of humour, laughter and good cheer. In an interview he gave
in 1991, Dr Fry concluded, 'Humour makes one a different
person. The power of effect doesn't stop below the neck . . .
mirth is accompanied by perturbations throughout the
body. Our very biology, our physical being, is touched. We
are strummed like a large guitar.'

Dr Fry describes laughter as a 'total body experience' in
which all the major systems of the body such as the muscles,
nerves, heart, brain and digestion participate fully. The
overall physical effect of laughter takes place, on the whole,
in two steps:

Step one: healthy stimulation;
Step two: deep relaxation.

First, with the advent of mirth, your body is manipulated
and exercised; second, during the afterglow of mirth, your
body becomes relaxed and soothed. Such is the profound

effect of this two-step reaction that laughter is sometimes called *internal massage*!

Dr Fry says that laughter is a good aerobic exercise that ventilates the lungs and leaves muscles, nerves and heart warm and relaxed. His research also demonstrates that laughter, like physical exercise, speeds up heart rate, steps up blood-pressure, quickens the breathing, expands circulation and enhances oxygen intake and expenditure.

During especially bubbly bouts of belly-laughter, Dr Fry's research demonstrates that laughter exercises not only the upper torso, lungs and heart but also certain muscle groups in the shoulders, arms, abdomen, diaphragm and legs. So pronounced are these effects that Dr Fry goes so far as to say that 100 to 200 laughs a day is the equivalent to about 10 minutes of rowing or jogging. This is indeed a wonderful message of hope for all of the failed joggers in the world – of which I am one!

Laughter and relaxation enjoy their own intimate relationship: laughter inspires relaxation; relaxation inspires laughter. The famous nineteenth-century philosopher Herbert Spencer was one of the first 'serious' scientists who alluded to the massaging effect of laughter, in his 1860 work *The Physiology of Laughter*. He believed that laughter serves as a wonderful safety-valve for coping with an 'overflow of nerve force' and for discharging 'disagreeable muscular motion'. He was convinced that laughter is an essential mechanism for restoring physical comfort, biological harmony and internal order.

In an article for *Psychology Today* (October 1987), Patricia Long reported the work of Sabina White at the University of California at Santa Barbara. In an effort to study the calming effect of laughter, Sabina White first asked 87 students to solve a mathematics paper crammed with very testing, trying problems and equations. Immediately afterwards the students were invited to listen to relaxation cassettes and to watch selected *Candid Camera* clips. Both relaxation and laughter helped to enhance circulation, relax muscle tension, soothe the sympathetic nervous system and regulate heart rate.

Other similar trials point out that it is not only the action of laughter that can help a person to relax, release and generally let go of tension; smiling, amusement, hopefulness and joyful feelings towards others and happy feelings of acceptance and worth for oneself can also inspire and enhance an 'all-over-feeling' of relaxation, 're-creation' and rest. A happy, relaxed frame of mind offers an ideal environment for allowing the body to create and enjoy a physical, chemical and biological balance, harmony and order.

One very important reason why laughter affects such profound relaxation for the whole body has to do with the effect of laughter on respiration. E. L. Lloyd, in his paper 'The Respiratory Mechanism in Laughter' (*Journal of General Psychology* 1938), showed that laughter usually commences with a long, drawn-out exhalation. Throughout an episode of laughter our exhalations are most often a little longer than our inhalations. During the 'recovery period' after laughter we are often forced to take in and to exhale long, slow, deep breaths. The action of this 'happy breathing', which is a combination of deep inhalation and full exhalation, will often inspire excellent ventilation, wonderful rest and profound release.

COMIC RELIEF FOR PAIN

Laughter is higher than all pain.
Elbert Hubbard

When Norman Cousins found out he had only a 1 in 500 chance of recovering from a sudden, mysterious spinal disease called ankylosing spondylitis he obviously had very little to laugh about. Within days his body had dramatically degenerated to the point that he had difficulty moving his limbs, his sleep was interrupted by incessant, crippling pain and his jaws became almost locked so that he could hardly speak.

In his now-famous article for the *New England Journal of Medicine* (December 1976), Cousins tells of his amazing recovery, first inspired by 'the joyous discovery that 10 minutes' of genuine belly-laughter had an anaesthetic effect and would give me at least two hours of pain-free sleep'. Cousins went on to explain that 'When the painkilling effect of the laughter wore off we would switch on the motion picture projector again and, not infrequently, it would lead to another pain-free sleep interval. Sometimes the nurse would read to me out of a trove of humor books. Especially useful were E.B. and Katherine White's *Subtreasury of American Humor* and Max Eastman's *The Enjoyment of Laughter*.'

Cousins is generally recognized today as the leading luminary of laughter medicine. His books *Anatomy of an Illness*, *The Healing Heart* and *Head First: The Biology of Hope* have enjoyed popular acclaim around the world from public, press and health professionals alike. In recognition of his courage, conviction and various efforts on behalf of laughter medicine, Cousins was made an adjunct professor in the School of Medicine at the University of California at Los Angeles (UCLA). His pioneering work in humour therapy, mind/body medicine and the role of positive emotions and immunity is very well respected indeed.

In a fascinating research paper entitled 'Effects of Laughter and Relaxation on Discomfort Thresholds' (*Journal of Behavioural Medicine* 1987), Cogan et al. describe two experiments conducted to test the proposal that laughter is a pain antagonist. In the first experiment, 20 male and 20 female subjects had 'pressure-induced discomfort' measured after they had each listened to, first, a 20-minute laughter cassette, second, a 20-minute relaxation cassette and third, a 20-minute dull, narrative cassette, or no cassette at all. Discomfort thresholds were found to be higher for subjects after the laughter cassette and relaxation cassette experiences.

In the second experiment, 40 female subjects went through a similar clinical text. Comic relief for pain was once again clearly evidenced. The authors concluded that, 'Discomfort thresholds increased for subjects in the laughter-inducing condition. Laughter, and not simply distraction, reduces discomfort sensitivity, suggesting that laughter has potential as an intervention strategy for the reduction of clinical discomfort.'

While laughter cannot cure pain, it is evident that laughter can help to facilitate genuine pain release. The ability of laughter to relax muscle tension and to soothe sympathetic nervous system stress can certainly help to promote pain control. Deeper breathing and an enhanced circulation, as inspired by laughter, can also help to minimize pain.

Best of all, perhaps, is the medical research that has found that a burst of buoyant belly-laughter can activate a release of two neuropeptide chemicals: *endorphins* and *enkephalins*. Both are commonly described as the body's natural pain-suppressing agents.

LAUGHTER ENERGY

Laughter is a most healthful exertion.
Christoph Wilhelm Hufeland

Laughter is a cheap, highly economical, ozone-friendly form of energy which can activate and animate the whole of your physical anatomy. As the British naturalist Charles Darwin so acutely observed in his 1872 masterpiece *The Expression of the Emotions in Man and Animals*, when we laugh 'circulation becomes more rapid; the eyes are bright and the colour of the face rises. The brain being stimulated by the increased flow of blood, reacts on the mental powers.' Laughter lends itself so well to life.

Laughter is sometimes described as a form of *eustress*, which is Hans Selye's term for positive, life-enhancing types of pressure, or stress. Laughter is a eustress because, unlike the physical effects of anger or anxiety where the body's supply of the chemical energy agents *adrenalin* and *noradrenalin* can run and run and run until burnout, laughter seems to have this built-in balancing mechanism that encourages the two-step action (stimulation, relaxation) mentioned above.

The action of laughter also releases *catecholamines*, which, together with adrenalin and noradrenalin, are thought to enhance blood flow, reduce inflammation, speed the healing process and heighten the overall arousal of the body. You can begin to see why laughter can be considered a serious therapeutic intervention.

'LIGHT-HEARTEDNESS'

A merry heart doeth good like a medicine; but a broken spirit drieth the bones.
Proverbs 17:22

Laughter, sometimes described as 'sunshine of the breast', certainly does seem to support the health of the heart muscle.

There is now a large library of medical research papers that have recorded how so-called 'negative emotions' such as unattenuated anger, high anxiety and personal stress can send heart rate racing and blood-pressure rising, sometimes to a fatal degree; while there is very little research on the potential impact of so-called 'positive emotions' such as happiness and love, Kaye Herth, RN, MSN, presented an interesting case history in an article entitled 'Laughter, a Nursing RX' (*American Journal of Nursing*, August 1984).

In this article she tells the story of a 'Mr L' whose moderate hypertension was uncontrolled despite medication and dietary restrictions. Kaye Herth gave 'Mr L' what she calls a 'funny bone history', which is partly designed to see how a person can incorporate laughter into a busy life schedule. 'We scheduled "laughter breaks" during which he would view his favourite videotapes (Bob Hope programmes). After two weeks his blood-pressure fell to within recommended limits. Undoubtedly a combination of factors contributed to his newly achieved control, but I believe the "laughter breaks" helped, too.'

LAUGHTER, STRESS AND IMMUNITY

Contentment preserves one even from catching cold. Has a woman who knew that she was well dressed ever caught a cold? – No, not even when she had scarcely a rag to her back.

Friedrich Wilhelm Nietzsche

Dr Lee S. Berk has done more than perhaps any other physician to further the case for laughter as a potential cloak of immunity. Again and again Dr Berk and his various research teams have discovered fascinating new evidence of the apparent role of laughter in physical, chemical and biological immunity. This research, above any other, has for modern medicine potentially the most serious, happy and far-reaching consequences of all.

One of the essential aims of Dr Berk's work has been to test whether positive emotional activities can act as modifiers of the particular hormones that are involved in the classical stress response. In a series of experiments, each involving five experimental subjects who viewed a 60-minute humour video and five control subjects who did not, Berk and his colleagues' measurements of mirthful laughter certainly provided the hypothesis: the laughter effect can counteract the stress effect.

In one of these experiments, reported in a paper for *Clinical Research* (1989) and entitled 'Eustress of Mirthful Laughter Modifies Natural Killer Cell Activity', Dr Berk and his colleagues found that 'mirthful laughter may attenuate some classical stress-related hormones and modify natural killer cell activity. Thus, this eustress or positive emotion may be capable of immunomodulation. In other words, it is possible that, as Nietzsche so humorously postulated, "Contentment preserves one even from catching cold." '

Dr Berk's findings are supported by the work of Dr S. M. Labott, who studied the chemical and biological impact of laughter and tears in 39 women who viewed sad and humorous videotapes. In his paper for the *Journal of Behavioural Medicine* (Winter 1990) entitled 'The Physiological and Psychological Effects of the Expression and Inhibition of Emotion', Dr Labott concluded, 'The humorous stimulus resulted in improved immunity, regardless of the overt laughter expressed.'

Similarly, there is recent research that suggests that people who regularly use laughter, humour and play as coping strategies for everyday events have a significantly higher count of the immunity antibody *immunoglobulin A* (IgA). As reported in the magazine *Well-being*, one study at Canada's University of Waterloo 'which rated people on their senses of humor, found that those who received higher scores in that category were found to also have higher levels of IgA and

IgG [also an immunoglobulin].' Norman Cousins points out that laughter has a role to play, not only in chemical and biological immunity but in mental and emotional immunity also. In an article for *Prevention* magazine (March 1988), Norman Cousins spoke of how he believes 'It is possible that laughter serves as a blocking agent. Like a bullet-proof vest, it may help protect you against the ravages of negative emotion that can assault you in disease.'

Occasionally, laughter and merriment can help to disperse the clouds of fear, worry, upset and self-doubt that can so often delay or deny a patient's full recovery. In these days of high-tech medical science, the positive health benefits of laughter remind us that there is also an art to medicine and that a part of this art requires health professionals to attend to body, mind and soul – to the *whole person*. This holistic method of health care offers the most helpful and hopeful of all approaches to immunity.

LAUGHTER MEDICINE AT WORK

Happy Hospitals

The art of medicine consists of amusing the patient while Nature cures the disease.

Voltaire

Some hospitals are no place to be ill in! Cold, damp corridors, dull, dark wards, the overpowering stench of disinfectant, walls without decoration, undervalued staff, exhausted doctors, non-nutritional meals, dishwater tea and coffee and a broken down old telly with no aerial are commonplace experiences. Too many hospitals are in danger of violating what the legendary 'lady of the lamp', nurse

Florence Nightingale described as the first principle of hospital care: 'A hospital should do the sick no harm.'

The Prince of Wales made a most telling observation of hospital life in his famous, controversial documentary for BBC television in 1988. 'It can't be easy to be healed in a soul-less concrete box,' he asserted, 'with characterless windows, inhospitable corridors and purely functional wards. The spirit needs healing as well as the body. Perhaps the greatest mistake of hospitals is that they cater for "patients" and not "people" – "whole people" with emotional, mental and spiritual needs as well as physical needs.'

An array of adventurous, innovative health care programmes have surfaced around the world in recent years as part of a collective effort to make hospitals more hospitable. These creative health care projects offer an apothecary of human medicines such as kindness, joy, fun and play. They aim, in particular, to enhance the greatest potential medicine of all: the therapeutic relationship between health professional and patient. A doctor, nurse or any other health professional who is well-versed only in the sciences of medical technology will always be second-best compared to the physician who is also a master of the human touch.

COMEDY CARTS

Leslie Gibson, RN, is the creator of the Comedy Cart at Morton Plant Hospital in Clearwater, Florida, USA. This hospital humour service offers a sparkling selection of fun, games and entertainment for patients at the hospital. 'Being hospitalized puts people at the highest possible stress level,' says Leslie, who also believes that 'besides promoting healing, humour is an excellent diversionary tool for keeping patients' minds off their pain.'

Leslie defines therapeutic humour as 'any positive interaction that when used constructively will maintain, enhance or improve the physical or emotional well-being of the human species.' Her comedy cart offers six main humour tools:

1   a selection of comic audio cassettes;
2   a library of humorous books;
3   a comedy video collection;
4   cartoons;
5   an assortment of fun and games; and,
6   a costumes/drama/and/magic mix.

The success of Leslie's innovative idea has inspired many other health professionals to take humour as a therapeutic intervention very seriously.

HUMOUR ROOMS

Karyn Buxman, RN, is one of a handful of nurses who has helped to establish happy 'humour rooms' as a popular and respected health service in many American hospitals. Humour rooms, similar to comedy carts, offer a creative space for patients who wish to enjoy themselves back to health. In 1991, Karyn co-founded the *Journal of Nursing Jocularity* in an effort to achieve national and international recognition of humour as a powerful potential healing adjunct to modern medical health care science.

'The Living Room' at St Joseph's Hospital in Houston, Texas has inspired many health professionals to experiment with such 'fun rooms'. At St Joseph's, as well as the normal games, toys, videos and books they also put on live acts for their patients, featuring comedians, magicians and drama groups. This modern therapeutic innovation is an echo of the ancient Greek idea that 'entertainment is a medicine.'

LAUGHTER CLINICS

The work of Dr Dhyan Sutorius at The Centre in Favour of Laughter in Amsterdam enjoys popular reviews throughout

Europe. He describes laughter as a 'transforming force' capable of prompting a greater physical, psychological and spiritual poise and balance in people. Dr Sutorius' centre is one of a growing network of professional health projects throughout Europe committed to laughter medicine, which also includes my own NHS Laughter Clinic at the West Birmingham Health Authority in England.

THE WORLD'S FIRST SILLY HOSPITAL

One of the most remarkable medical centres is the Gesundheit Institute run by family doctor and performing clown Hunter D. (Patch) Adams, MD, in Arlington, Virginia, USA. Patch charges no medical fees, relies entirely upon voluntary donations and carries no malpractice insurance. 'The best therapy is being happy,' he insists, 'All the other things doctors can do are, at best, aids.' His colleagues allow themselves to be 'happy, funny, loving, co-operative and creative' with patients. Thousands have benefited from Patch Adam's philosophy and practice, in which both humour and human contact are encouraged to play their full curative roles.

SEND IN THE CLOWNS

The seventeenth-century English physician Thomas Sydenham, often referred to as the 'English Hippocrates', caused consternation among his colleagues when he once said, 'The arrival of a happy clown exercises a more beneficial influence upon the health of a town than of 20 asses laden with drugs.' Leon 'Jo-Jo' Laurence is Public Relations Officer for Clowns International, the world's oldest surviving club for clowns. He and his clown colleagues have on many occasions been invited to hospital wards to raise good cheer among the patients.

Leon recently wrote to me with a marvellous story of how 'today, following one of my shows, a lady rushed up to my clown partner and myself and kissed us all over as she told us how much our show had heartened her so. Times had apparently been tough for this kind lady who told us how for months she had been afraid to go out and was on the point of nervous breakdown. During the first part of our show she had felt nothing, but as the show went on she told us how she surprised herself first by smiling and then by beginning to laugh. "I feel strong again," she told us. Send in the clowns! Send in the clowns!'

Michael 'Dr Stubs' Christensen realized a delightful dream in 1986 when he founded the Big Apple Circus Clown Care Unit in New York. In an interview for the Institute for the Advancement of Health publication *Mind-Body Health Digest* (vol. 4, no. 2, 1990), he told how in less than five years his circus developed into a network of 24 clowns in eight city hospitals, making it the largest hospital clowning programme in the world. 'This is the most rewarding performing I've ever done,' said Michael, 'Our only task is to make patients feel good. We have no agenda, and that includes laughter. Sometimes it's enough just to be there.'

HOSPITAL 'RADIO-HO-HO'

This is a wonderful potential humour therapy for hospital environments. A happy blend of music, chat and comedy can offer a definite therapeutic value. Some hospitals in the US are now experimenting with a hospital video comedy channel for their patients. A happy hospital ward is one of the essential inspirations for a healthy hospital ward.

Month by month there is always news of innovative, humanistic health care initiatives starting up, such as decorating hospital wards with 'happy colours'; enlisting singers, pianists and professional music therapists; experiencing the 'healing joy' of dogs, cats, parrots and fish as part of 'pet-facilitated' therapy programmes; and enlisting the support of local comedians, amateur impersonators and drama students. All of these creative enterprises are inspired by a basic belief that the quality of his or her stay in hospital can help a patient along the road to better health and a better life.

The principal aim of these various creative health projects is not laughter; rather, laughter is a tool that serves the greater aim of liberating the human spirit. The greatest resources for health are human ones, resources inspired and activated by the powers of happiness, hope, optimism, self-worth and a positive desire for well-being. Humour gives us heart; humour gives us hope. Laughter is a lamp that dispels the shadows cast by illness.

Laughter is one tool, human contact is another; there are other creative healing tools such as music therapy, art therapy, colour therapy, pet-facilitated therapy, game-playing and clowning, all of which can work with technical medical interventions to provide an effective, exhilarating 'whole-help' programme for personal health, harmony and happiness. Essentially put, laughter reminds us not to leave the spirit out of medicine.

LAUGHTER MEDICINE FOR HEALTH PROFESSIONALS

Physician, be happy thyself
Luke 4:23 (slightly amended!)

Even health professionals are now helping themselves to humour workshops, laughter lectures and smile-power seminars. Training and education programmes with titles such as 'Jest for the Health of It', 'The Joy of Caring', 'The Nurse Who Laughs, Lasts', 'Ho-Ho-Holistic Health Care' and 'Doctor, I Feel Funny' are becoming increasingly popular in a demanding profession where nurses, doctors, therapists, counsellors and social workers will often use humour quite naturally as a line of defence.

Nurse co-ordinator Stephanie Ferguson, MS, RN, is adamant that 'Humour is one of the basic human needs that nurses must consider when assessing, planning and implementing care.' Humour can be a therapeutic tool for creating healthy relationships between patient and health professional. As Maggie Kuhn, the American writer, once humorously observed, 'The ultimate indignity is to be given a bedpan by a stranger who calls you by your first name.' Humour in health care settings is often needed to alleviate fear, uncertainty and moments of awkwardness; humour can also enhance the mutual trust, confidence and faith between patient and carer. Health care models that advocate detached, distanced and impersonal technical nursing styles are quite clearly inadequate. Patients may well require medical science for their body, but they also need human kindness, love and understanding for their mind, emotions and soul.

Health professionals are not required to be stand-up comedians, impressionists or occasional cabaret artists. As Dr Joel Goodman (founder of the Humor Project in the US) says, 'There's a myth in the health care field that every physician is now supposed to be a comic too. Humor as a health intervention is not about gags, jokes and punch-lines. It's an attitude, a way of being open, a gentle embracing of reality. We encourage professionals to invite smiles and laughter, not to try to make patients laugh.'

The increasing incidence of stress-related illness and burnout among health professionals is a major cause for concern. After all, if a medical system cannot care adequately for its own staff, how can that same system expect to care for its patients? The health, happiness and wholeness of health professionals are fundamental for promoting the health, happiness and wholeness of patients. Gradually, the health profession is learning to care for the carers, providing much needed workshops and training on successful stress control, relaxation strategies, assertion techniques and, also, laughter.

Dr Patch Adams travels the world giving training to health professionals. In his 'The Joy of Caring' workshops he tells professional carers, 'I do not believe burnout is inherent in medical practice. In fact, I experience just the opposite. The practice of medicine is a breathtaking thrill – love exchanged in so fundamental a way that it is difficult to contain the excitement . . . If we are to address the cost of care and burnout, I think it is necessary that we direct our focus towards wellness and creating a living friendship between doctor and patient.'

Humour, happiness and health are interdependent. Humour and happiness inspire and promote physical, emotional and spiritual health; humour and happiness are often the most cherished rewards of health; humour and happiness between patient and carer can enhance a patient's progress towards health; and, as some health professionals are now discovering, humour and happiness are essential tools of survival for a career in health. Everybody can enjoy the benefits of happiness, even health professionals!

Laughter medicine offers a positive and practical way of *living life, loving life and laughing with life*, together. Laughter is the 'X' on the map where our buried treasure lies.

LAUGHTER MEDICINE EXERCISES

He who laughs best today, will also laugh last.
Friedrich Wilhelm Nietzsche

At the Laughter Clinic we have a motto: 'The most wasted day is that in which we have not laughed.'

The following laughter medicine exercises are among the most popular creative growth games we play at the Laughter Clinic. Each exercise offers you an opportunity to

1 laugh for laughter's sake and
2 use laughter as a catalyst for exploring other jewels in life's treasure chest, such as the powers of creativity, joy, love, happiness and hope.

The theories of laughter medicine are good; the practice is even better!

COMIC VISION

The 'perception principle' warns *be careful what you look for, for it will find you*. Thus a cynic tends to see only the headlines that herald bad news, a hypochondriac finds only illness and evidence of new ailments, and an optimist discovers wonder, amusement and hope almost everywhere. Life is full of laughter, if we will but look for it. Comic vision teaches us to look not just with our eyes but also with our thoughts, attitudes, feelings and beliefs for all that is funny, joyful and delightful in our daily lives.

To practise comic vision, choose one day of your life to make a written record of every humorous and joyful event, witticism, instance of word play, you have the privilege of witnessing or hearing personally. Do this once, twice, three times and you will find, as Joel Goodman so rightly says, 'If you look for humour, humour will find you.'

HAPPY BREATHING I

Happy breathing is a 'portable' exercise that can inspire relaxation, calm and confidence, anywhere and at any time.

We breathe very differently when we are happy and when we are sad. 'Sad' breathing tends to be a very shallow, sporadic and stressful, causing tension in the heart and anxiety in the mind. 'Happy' breathing is, by contrast, full, flowing and regular; it creates a wonderful harmony between energy intake on the inhalation and tension release on the exhalation. Laughter encourages this type of happy breathing.

To perform happy breathing, begin by focusing your attention on the rhythm of your breath. Whenever your mind wanders, just bring it back to your breathing. Now, with every single breath you take, breathe more fully, allowing the breath to flow freely.

You can, if you wish, enhance this exercise by performing a simulated smile (see below) with every other out-breath.

SIMULATED SMILES

The time to smile is when you really need to smile. The 'simulated smile', or pretend grin, is a calculated act of defiance, a symbol of unswerving positive intention and an unmistakable gesture of inner resolve, designed to welcome future happiness and to stamp a seal of veritable victory over the current stresses in your life.

Simulated smiling is a joyful version of the popular coping strategy known as 'acting as if' – that is, if you want to feel happy, *act* happy. Don't suppress your sadness: just feel the sadness and act happy anyway! A full session of simulated smiling can last anywhere from three seconds to three minutes. You may even, if you wish, add a 'ha, ha, ha' and maybe even move on to more orchestrated and elaborate guffaws. Simulated smiles often stimulate the real thing!

TRANSCENDENTAL CHUCKLING

This is the silliest of all the creative growth games that we play at the Laughter Clinic.

To perform transcendental chuckling you should, on waking each morning, sit in a cross-legged, upright position before a mirror and embark upon two minutes of laughing for no reason whatsoever. Life will never be the same. Anyone who sends a tape of his or her two minutes' unconditional laughter to the Laughter Clinic receives a Certificate of Membership to the Happy Human Being Club. Now *there*'s an incentive!

The aim is to achieve an expression of pure, unblocked joviality that will set you up for a day of joy. To perform this exercise well you have to transcend and laugh through some of the self-criticism, seriousness and unhappy belief systems that so often get in the way of pure, spontaneous joy.

FUN TIME

The comedian Woody Allen once said, 'Most of the time I don't have much fun, the rest of the time I don't have any fun at all.' How true is that for you? What do you do for fun? Do you ever short-change yourself on fun time? Are you waiting around for the fun to start? How long are you prepared to wait?

Laughter, fun and play are most marvellous medicines for helping us rejuvenate ourselves as well as relax and radiate calm. Regular intervals of fun time and social recreation are essentials that can promote personal health, happy relationships, joyful work habits and a high-quality style of life. Treat yourself to some fun today! Remember, it's now or never.

DONATE A SMILE TO A WORTHY CAUSE

This is a 'sweet charity' Laughter Clinic campaign that is designed to exercise the smile muscles in your face (and your heart!). Smiles are a universal currency. A greater expenditure of smiles will, if invested wisely, reap many rich dividends for you.

To donate a smile to a worthy cause, the very first thing you must decide is who or what shall be among your worthy causes! Start making your list now. Most people often identify loved ones as worthy causes. Some people get very adventurous and donate their smiles to pets, to plants, to their car and even to traffic wardens, taxmen and accountants!

Of course, the donation does not necessarily need to be a smile; it may be something else you give, like a 'thank you', a cheerful 'hello' or flowers – any of which might actually invite smiles in return. The desired effect of this adventurous campaign is that perhaps, on one special day, we may all donate together so that we light up the whole world with a smile!

CHUCKLING TAPES

A ready supply of infectious laughter (or 'laughter music' as I call it) coming from the speakers of your home hi-fi, your car cassette-deck or your personal stereo is a novel, effective way to amuse yourself. Variations on this theme also include bags of joy, toys of laughter, the 'Laughing Policeman' song or even a recording of your own transcendental chuckling, for instance. Occasional injections of infectious laughter can keep you immune from morbidity, misery and other mental mumbo-jumbo.

LAUGHTER LOG

Creating and maintaining a 'laughter log' of your life in which you record 'happy highlights' of each day is a truly delightful experience. Jokes, celebrations, witty sayings, humorous anecdotes, joyful events, entertainments, funny moments, slip-ups, successes, thrills, moments of inspiration (also known as *eurekas!*), romantic adventures and silly stories can all make excellent entries. In no time at all your laughter log will become a most precious transcript of your personal history – a true blessing.

LAUGHTER LIBRARY

A library of joke books, classic cartoon annuals, collections of humorous quotations, audio cassettes of your favourite comedians, highly prized comedy videos, enjoyable board games, toys, fun-and-game books, comic plays and novels and amusing biographies (just some examples) are all happy assets for any home. Your laughter library will be an oasis to comfort, rejuvenate, divert and inspire you in times of need.

THE JOKER CARD

'Give and you shall receive' is an old bit of wisdom that has been around for centuries, mainly because it's true! If you want happiness, spread happiness; if you want love, spread love; and if you want laughter, spread laughter. Most emotions are highly infectious. If you make an effort to radiate happiness, love and laughter, you will be in a better position to receive these gifts from others.

Make an effort to play The Joker Card at least once a day so that at least one person somewhere will enjoy a taste of happiness, love and laughter as a result of your efforts.

3

HUMOUR, HAPPINESS AND HEALTH

We don't laugh because we're happy – we're happy because we laugh.

William James

Allowing yourself to develop naturally the humour, laughter and fun in your life and to expand your experience of personal happiness can certainly help to enhance and enrich your health. Health flourishes in a happy environment.

'HO-HO-HOLISTIC MEDICINE'

For the last few centuries or so doctors have been trained for the most part to practise medicine as a 'serious science' and not as a 'happy art'. The mechanistic, reductionist scientist has become preoccupied with a 'body-only' theory of medicine that muses over miniature universes of muscles, nerves, tissues and cells. There has been no place for the mind, the soul, or for the human touch.

The masters of ancient medicine had no microscopes, optical fibre cameras or microchip technology. The moods, feelings, temperament and disposition (happy or unhappy) of a patient were considered the critical indicators. Physicians of long ago identified four cardinal 'humours' – physical fluids or moistures believed to be associated with different moods and to affect the balance of health: yellow bile (or choler) equalled anger, black bile (or melancholy) was associated with sadness, phlegm with lassitude, blood with optimism. Too much phlegm or not enough choler, therefore, might upset a person's overall physical, mental, emotional and spiritual well-being. Balance was the key. When a person fell ill, the physician would 'humour the patient' back to balance, and health.

How the medical establishment ever forgot that both mind and body contribute to sickness, health and well-being is a mystery. Even today, there are still some 'experts' who persist with the notion that mind and body live separate, unconnected lives.

Scientific research into psychosomatic medicine has proved beyond a shadow of a doubt that people can become 'worried sick'. Over the past half-decade approximately 25,000 research papers, articles and textbooks have recorded a catalogue of unhealthy bodily reactions to negative emotions such as anger, anxiety, depression and fear. Psychosomatic medicine has established that every event of the mind creates a corresponding echo in the organs, systems and passageways of the body. The body is not merely a vehicle: it is a territory of the unconscious mind and a map of the conscious mind. The mind/body medicine concept is scientifically proven; the search for 'how', 'what', 'where', 'when' and 'why' is now gathering speed.

Stress is arguably the main cause of illness in modern life. Research into the stress effect and stress-related illnesses incorporates a 'full person', mind/body model of medicine. Blood-pressure, heart rate, respiration levels, muscle tension, nerves, brainwaves and body temperature, for instance, have all been found to react adversely to the negative use of emotion during stressful encounters. Stress is a mind/body phenomenon.

If negative emotions can have a potential negative effect on the health of the body, then could it be that positive emotions can have a potentially positive effect on the health of the body? Could happiness and humour, as well as laughter, enhance harmony and health? This would only seem to be common sense.

Perhaps the most exciting area of mind/body research is the science of psycho-neuro-immunology (PNI), or psycho-neuro-endocrine-immunology, to use its fuller name! PNI studies the free-flowing communication and interaction between mind, brain and immune system. The initial studies seem to suggest that people can make themselves either psychologically immune or psychologically prone to physical illnesses. While I served as assistant editor to the complementary health journal *Caduceus*, I had the pleasure of working on a marvellous article by Roger J. Booth, a Senior Research Fellow in the Department of Immunobiology at Auckland University School of Medicine. He concluded in his article, entitled 'Psychoneuroimmunology' (Winter 1990), 'Immunologists can no longer consider the immune system in isolation from the rest of the body-mind-spirit and must seriously address the possibility that if diseases can be dramatically influenced by "state of mind", then perhaps altering a "state of mind" may be more beneficial than intervening solely at the level of the immune system.'

PNI claims that happiness, humour and a healthy use of joyful emotions can offer potential psychological immunity to possible physical illnesses and upsets. Maybe the time has come to expand the holistic model of health into a 'ho-ho-holistic' one that actively encourages the interrelationship of health, happiness, humour and wholeness.

HUMOUR PSYCHOLOGY

The great majority of schools of psychology, counselling and psychotherapy have pursued a 'heavy/serious, problem-orientated approach' to mental health. If you were to look in the index of many of the leading psychology textbooks you would often find key words missing, such as 'happiness', 'humour', 'laughter', 'hope', 'joy' and 'love'. Indeed, for every 500 papers published on the negative, harmful effects of emotional disturbance, there are only approximately four or five papers published on the positive, healthy effects of emotional experiences such as laughter. Psychologists seem to enjoy studying neuroses, psychoses, hysteria, depression and phobias much more than exploring happiness, joy, love and laughter. Curious! Indeed, only a relative handful of psychologists have, through the centuries, amused and bemused themselves with a study of laughter.

In total there are now some 80 differing and contrasting theories as to why humans laugh. Most psychologists can agree only that laughter is a mystery – and one that may never be totally fathomed. Many, however, will admit that moments of humour can occur quite frequently during consultation and therapy sessions. Most of these professionals appear to take no serious note of these moments; a small handful will read into and ponder the meaning behind the humour; but only a very few will actually go out of their way to *use* humour as positive psychotherapeutic tools.

Sigmund Freud, for all his fixations on aggression and sex, made a point of studying jokes, humour and laughter. His 1928 written work *Jokes and their Relation to the Unconscious* expounds a fascinating 'tension-relief' theory for laughter which will be explored later in this chapter. Freud occasionally confessed he would use humour to make a point with patients.

Warren S. Poland MD, writing in the *Psychoanalytic Quarterly* (LIX, 1990), suggests,

> *Mature humour is a reflection of analytic work successfully done . . . [this] humour offers an opportunity for sustenance and consolation throughout life. Insightful humour not only has its 'given' aspects but is itself a gift, a gift the ego gives to itself. It offers self comfort without denial. Indeed, its mark is so precisely its capacity to soothe while at the same time respecting the power of inner conflicts and outer hurts. The facilitating of the development of the patient's capacity for mature humour is one of the happiest and proudest effects of clinical analysis.*

Alfred Adler, founder of Individual Psychology, was serious about laughter. His famous phrase, 'If we make ourselves smile, we actually feel like smiling' highlights an important principle of psychology.

Viktor Frankl, a student of Freud's, developed a school of psychotherapy called *logotherapy* – nicknamed 'the third Viennese school' (Freud's being the first and Adler's the second) – which also incorporated humour as a central part of therapy. Frankl encouraged his patients not to 'fight or flee' their problems but to have fun with them instead. Viktor Frankl's nephew, Freddie Frankl, runs a private clinic in Birmingham, England, which promotes the jolly motto, 'One giggle is worth two tablets.'

Gestalt therapy, founded by Fritz Perls, reasons that humour can help to facilitate greater self-awareness, a happy self-acceptance and a better balance and integration of the whole Self. Gestalt therapists are encouraged to use appropriate humour to enhance therapy.

Transactional Analysis and existentialism are two more schools of counselling that recognize the potential benefits of laughter in therapy.

Laughter is a basic human need. Laughter is also a fundamental characteristic and attribute of a fully functioning person. The American psychologist Abraham Maslow, the founder of Client-centred therapy Carl Rogers, and the existential psychiatrist R.D. Laing are three well-respected pioneers of psychology who have held this view. Another is H. Greenwald, who once wrote 'When humour is significantly eliminated in a person's functioning, the path towards psychological growth is slowed.'

The fact that laughter is such a unique, individual and multi-functional behavior with many subtleties, vagaries and varieties has thwarted many psychologists' brave attempts to define, to describe and to record laughter in therapy. One attempt was that of J. Levine, who created a 'Mirth Response Test' in the 1950s to help diagnose neurotic and psychotic conditions. His patients' responses to cartoon drawings were measured on a six-point 'Mirth Spectrum' scale of 1) negative response, 2) no response, 3) half-smile; 4) smile; 5) chuckle; 6) laugh.

Dr Albert Ellis, founder of Rational Emotive Therapy (RET), has done more than anyone to give humour, laughter and fun their rightful places in psychotherapy. A central principle of RET is that people often disturb themselves with irrational, subjective, and over-serious thinking. Dr Ellis describes this thinking as 'catastrophizing'; 'awfulizing', 'terrible-izing' and 'horrible-izing'.

Dr Ellis also describes how people create dogmatic, non-humorous mental straitjackets for themselves by following illusionary 'oughts', 'shoulds' and 'musts'. In a lecture he gave at the American Psychological Association Convention in 1976, entitled 'Fun as Psychotherapy', he said,

Instead of mainly wanting, preferring and desiring various things and relationships, we frequently demand and command that we get them and insist that we absolutely must have them. With this kind of musterbation, *a form of behaviour infinitely more pernicious than masturbation, we render ourselves disturbed and seriously defeat ourselves.*

In the same lecture, Dr Ellis asked,

> *What better vehicle for doing some of this ideological uprooting than humour and fun? If neurotics take themselves, others and the world's conditions too solemnly, why not poke the blokes with jolly jokes!? . . . I use humour in many different ways with the aim of directly and forcibly attacking my clients' ideas; not, mind you, my clients, for one of the main tenets of RET consists of unconditionally accepting people with their mistakes and idiocies, of fully acknowledging their human fallibilities and pig-headedly refusing to condemn or damn them no matter what they do or don't do.*

The ability to laugh at oneself, in particular, is a vital psychological immunity against the modern thinking disease of 'over-seriousness'. Dr Ellis promotes laughter as a mental and emotional tool that can so often inspire a return to balanced, objective, rational thought. Dr Ellis's RET is a happiness-orientated therapy which aims not only to help a client to get rid of problems but also to employ methods and strategies that will help him or her grasp greater happiness and personal fulfilment.

Dr Ellis and others recognize that laughter can help to convey warmth, communicate commonality and strengthen the bond of empathy between counsellor and client. Laughter can also foster a client's hope, trust and confidence in his or her therapist. If the therapist can laugh and, thereby, show that he or she is human, then the client often gains faith in the 'goodness' of the therapist. As Thomas Carlyle once said, 'No person who has once heartily and wholly laughed can be altogether irreclaimably bad'!

Some psychologists quite rightly sound a note of caution. As the pioneer of humour in nursing, Vera Robinson RN, Ph.D., has pointed out, 'Humour becomes destructive and

dysfunctional when it abets pathological denial of reality.'
Laughter can be used in ways that are either healthful or
harmful – the potential is powerful, either way.

TYPES OF LAUGHTER AND THEIR USES

An absence of laughter is a classic sign of a person who is
becoming weighed down, snowed under and clouded over
by a perceived personal problem. Conversely, many people
will testify that the moment they were able to laugh at their
predicament was a significant turning point in their life. This
common experience of 'laughter as a turning point' was the
main inspiration for setting up my NHS Laughter Clinic.

Freud noted different types of humour such as 'hostile
humour' (wit), 'sexual humour' and 'empathic humour' –
each of which served a different function. Let's take a look
at some of the different kinds of laughter.

Comic Relief, or Relaxation Humour

*Humour is a whisper from the Soul, imploring mind and
body to relax, let go and be at peace again.*
Anonymous

Laughter helps us relax, forget for a while, loosen the
imposing and threatening grip of fear, dispel unwanted worry
and anxiety, and be more tolerant and accepting.

In the opening pages of my book *Stress Busters* I describe
life as a 'poignant, bittersweet affair, made from a mixed
marriage of both ups and downs, high points and low points,
happy times and sad times, smiles and frowns. Experience
can never be "all good" or "all bad" – it is, inevitably, a
mixture of both.' To use the vernacular of laughter medicine,

life is a tragi-comedy, a quirky combination of glory and grief, laughter and lows, joys and sorrows. As W. C. Fields once said, 'It's a funny old world – a man's lucky if he gets out of it alive!' The real challenge is to bless it all, enjoy it all and laugh with it all. Laughter can lighten the load!

Taking time out for laughter can be a wonderful way to unwind, take stock and just, simply, 'be'. As Joseph Addison once said, 'If we consider the frequent reliefs we receive from laughter, and how often it breaks the gloom which is apt to depress the mind, one would take care not to grow too wise for so great a pleasure in life.'

Escape Laughter, or Defence Humour

There cannot be a crisis next week. My schedule is already full.
Henry Kissinger

The rise of classic comedy cinema in the late 1920s and 1930s accelerated due to a demand for temporary escape from the day-to-day struggle of the living through the Great Depression. Laurel and Hardy, Harold Lloyd, Charlie Chaplin and the Marx Brothers, for example, offered people a chance to 'pack up your troubles in your old kit-bag, and smile, smile, smile'. Janice Anderson, in her marvellous book, *History of Movie Comedy*, explains how laughter and comedy gave people the opportunity to walk away from personal woes for a while. She goes on to say, 'More than just a tickling of the public's fancy, [great comedy] is a lightening of the dark places in men's souls, a noting of the fact that human nature is perhaps more misled, more ignorant or just plain lost than intentionally evil. Great comedy gives a glimmer of hope for the future of the human race.'

Laughter offers a very capable form of defence against the daily encounters of failure, upset, mistakes, errors, traumas and criticisms. Two of my favourite sayings in life are, 'I can take any amount of criticism, so long as it is unqualified praise,' by Noel Coward, and 'Honest criticism is hard to take, particularly from a relative, a friend, an acquaintance or a stranger,' by Franklin P. Jones. Both are classic examples of defence humour.

Sublimated Laughter, or Hostile Humour

He spoke with a certain what-is-it in his voice, and I could see that, if not actually disgruntled, he was far from gruntled.

P. G. Wodehouse

Not surprisingly, perhaps, it was Freud who came up with the idea of sublimated laughter, or hostile humour. He believed that laughter can help to thwart aggression, cool hostility and avoid violent conflict. Certain forms of humour, such as satire, sarcasm and irony, are safe, physically non-violent ways to communicate your annoyance or anger. Parents, teachers, schools, bosses, councils, governments and religions are frequent targets of sublimated humour.

In Erma Bombeck's classic read, *If Life is a Bowl of Cherries – What am I Doing in the Pits?* she writes, 'I read one psychologist's theory that said, "Never strike a child in anger." When *could* I strike him? When he is kissing me on my birthday? When he is recuperating from measles? Do I slap the Bible out of his hand on a Sunday?' This is a great example of sublimated humour – laughing off, instead of lashing out!

Sublimated laughter can be (mis)used in a very hurtful, cutting way. The best type of laughter is laughter *with* someone, not *at* someone. If, however, you find your anger is eating you up and you are in danger of manifesting a mental ulcer, then laughter at is better than clubbing someone. 'You are not angry with people when you laugh at them. Humour teaches tolerance' – there is some truth in these words of Somerset Maugham.

Surprise Laughter, or Incongruity Humour

Anything awful makes me laugh. I misbehaved once at a funeral.

Charles Lamb

Laughter is a safety valve that, once opened, can allow us to release the tension that can generate so rapidly during moments of shock, surprise, incongruity and the unexpected. Often we will laugh not because we are enjoying ourselves but because we find ourselves in a 'funny-strange' situation. By being able to 'laugh it off' we gain valuable space, time and opportunity to gather our thoughts. Laughter facilitates adaptation.

When we study the anatomy of jokes we find that many jokes rely on an element of shock or incongruity. John Dewey describes laughter as 'the pleasure of suddenly attaining unity [or understanding] at the end of a period of suspense'. This is how most jokes run. For example:

Why do surgeons wear masks during operations?

– So that no one will know which one of them made the mistake.

Shock and surprise!

Two men who quite clearly have had a fixation on sex are Sigmund Freud and Woody Allen. Freud spent a lot of time studying 'naughty' humour, which uses sexual innuendo and sprightly obscenities. He felt that this humour created laughter because of its 'shock value': the naughty jokes are not innately funny; the shock of them is. Woody Allen once said, 'I believe that sex is a beautiful thing between two people. Between five, it's fantastic!' On another occasion he reflected, 'Is sex dirty? Only if it's done right!' This is shock humour.

Perception Laughter, or Observation Humour

I have a new philosophy. I'm going to dread only one day at a time.

Charles Schultz, *Peanuts*

Many of the greatest comedy writers have either consciously or unconsciously followed a golden comedy rule: to change perceptions. Taking something ordinary, familiar and commonplace and then turning it upside-down offers a wonderful potential for comedy. The Monty Python team did this all the time! They invited us in to an ordinary pet shop, which sold dead parrots; they showed us a normal government ministry, for silly walks!; they filmed a commonplace athletics event, with a 100-metre dash for people with a poor sense of direction!

Joel Goodman (of the Humor Project) says, 'There are two ways to look at things: Life is a serious matter; life is a laughing matter.' You can choose either perspective at any given time. By laughing at events of life, instead of running away, for instance, we do see things differently. When we see differently, we feel differently and we behave differently. In other words, when we change our perception of reality, reality changes. Laughter is often the catalyst that makes this change possible. Psychologists occasionally use the term *insightful humour* to describe the function of humour in focusing our objectivity and balance.

Shared Laughter, or Bonding Humour

Laughter is the best way to make somebody's heart beat.
R. Holden

Shared laughter can help people find common ground. Even the very best friendships can become awkward without the odd smile or humorous exchange. Laughter can help to heal and enhance our relationship with ourselves and our relationship with others.

Humour can be misused to highlight differences, distances and separateness. Racial jokes, cultural jokes (as between 'Aussies' and 'Poms'), national jokes ('English' and 'Irish') and sexist jokes (about 'dumb blondes', for instance) all emphasize differences and dis-unity. They also reveal a certain amount of ignorance. Once again, though, humour is not innately good or bad – rather, it is our use of it that takes it one way or the other.

Triumphant Laughter, or Superiority Humour

Humour is an affirmation of dignity, a declaration of man's superiority to all that befalls him.
Romain Gary

Laughter encourages us to confront and tackle stressful subjects in a safe and socially acceptable way. When we laugh at ourselves and our personal dilemmas it can help us to rise above things and 'come up smiling'. This type of laughter empowers us and is most often called superiority humour.

Many of the world's favourite comedians work on the superiority theory of humour. By adopting an inferior standpoint they help us, the audience, to feel superior. Woody Allen, for one: his stand-up persona is inferior and neurotic; we are superior, safe and sound. Some comedians work together, one inferior, the other superior. Laurel and Hardy, Abbott and Costello, Bob Hope and Bing Crosby, Morecambe and Wise all spring to mind.

Psychologists such as Adler tend to use the word 'superiority' to describe strength, mastery and victory not so much over others but over our own feelings, thoughts and dilemmas – and ultimately over our selves. The philosopher Thomas Hobbes described laughter as 'the sudden glory arising from a dawning belief in some eminency in ourselves, by comparison with the infirmity of others, or, with our own former infirmity'.

Sigmund Freud described humour as an 'ego builder' and laughter as a potential 'triumph of the ego'. In *Jokes and their Relation to the Unconscious* he wrote of laughter: '[it is one of] the great series of methods which the human mind has constructed in order to evade the compulsion to suffer.' He added that through laughter 'a person refuses to suffer, emphasizes the invincibility of his ego by the real world, victoriously maintains the pleasure principle – and all this, in contrast to other methods having the same purposes, without overstepping the bounds of mental health.'

The key to the superiority theory of humour is that when we laugh we tend to feel good about ourselves, and when we feel good about ourselves it is much easier to feel good about our experiences, our future and our lives in general.

Affirmation Laughter, or Reinforcement Humour

Laugh, and the world laughs with you.
Ella Wheeler Wilcox

Perhaps the most obvious reason why we sometimes laugh is that we feel happy. Laughter reinforces the good feelings we have for ourselves, for others and for the world around us. And when we laugh, we feel like laughing again, and again. One of the mottos we live by at the Laughter Clinic is, 'If you are able to laugh a little it makes it easier to laugh a lot!'

Laughter has magical power. A single moment of laughter can change the shape of the world in an instant, endow us with the strength demanded by the moment, and alter our futures forever. Humour truly heals!

HAPPINESS IS . . .

Happiness is no laughing matter.
Richard Whately, nineteenth-century Archbishop of Dublin

The most important possession in life is a personal dictionary in which you define for yourself key words such as 'love', 'peace' 'health', 'wealth', 'success', 'spirituality', 'laughter' and 'happiness'. Everyone wants to taste happiness; only a few people, though, have ever sat down to work out what happiness means for them. If you don't know what happiness is, how do you expect to be happy?

'What's a joy to the one is a nightmare to the other. That's how it is today; that's how it'll be forever,' wrote the German dramatist, Bertolt Brecht. Psychologists, philosophers, theologians, sociologists, politicians and humorists mostly agree that happiness is a principal aim in life for us all; they mostly disagree as to what happiness is.

Is happiness a feeling or a thought, or both? Our perception of happiness is apt to change throughout the progress of our lives: what we describe as 'happy' one day may be 'nothing much' on another. Most people say, 'I'll know happiness when it happens,' to which I reply, 'Jolly Good! How long are you prepared to wait?' For many people the sad truth is usually the opposite: people do not know happiness when it happens; they only know happiness when it *has* happened – in other words, when it has gone. At the Laughter Clinic we make it our business to explore what happiness is, to define and describe what happiness does, and to live with happiness, now, as best we can.

One of the most popular workshops at the Laughter Clinic is *The Happiness Charter*. The purpose of The Happiness Charter is to define and describe what happiness is. We begin with the words, 'Happiness is . . .' and then go around the group, one by one, attempting to fill the blank with as many descriptions as possible. The usual initial reaction is bewilderment – and laughter! Many people have not thought about happiness in such a concentrated, focused and direct manner before.

The answers often range from the sublime to the ridiculous: 'Happiness is . . . feeling good about myself and others,' ' . . . a chocolate milkshake,' ' . . . the human touch,' ' . . . a Labour Government,' ' . . . an attitude of mind,' ' . . . health,' ' . . . loving and being loved,' ' . . . achieving goals' and ' . . . a hot bath with bubbles!'

HAPPINESS CHARTER

Happiness is an attitude. Happiness happens inside-out, not outside-in. There is no magical formula that states that X per cent of status or wealth will guarantee happiness. 'Happiness depends, as Nature shows/Less on exterior things than most suppose,' wrote William Cowper. To be happy, you must think yourself happy. Happiness is a product of mind, of attitude and of thought. Happiness comes *from* you, not *to* you.

Happiness is a perception. If you look for happiness, happiness will find you. Many people make themselves unhappy in life because they look for all the things in life they either haven't got or cannot have; they rarely take the time to look at, acknowledge and appreciate all that they have got. If you want to look for happiness, look no further than the end of your nose!

Happiness is a talent. Happiness is not a gift given to 'the chosen few'. Happiness is a talent and a skill. Happiness is like a muscle – it needs to be flexed and exercised. At the Laughter Clinic we believe that happiness happens if you let it. Happiness is only ever a thought/feeling away.

Happiness is now. Are you waiting to be happy 'if', 'after', 'only', 'when' or 'soon'? How long are you prepared to wait? Would you like to be happy, but feel you can't right now? We can look forward with optimism and joy to the future and we can look back with gratitude – but happiness can only ever happen in the *now*. 'I have the happiness of the passing moment, and what more can a mortal ask?' wrote George Gissing.

Happiness is a way of travelling. Happiness is not so much a final destination as a way of journeying through life. There is no need to 'save up' all your happiness for an event or goal somewhere into the distant future; look for happiness today, along the way, as you go. Benjamin Franklin got it right when he said, 'Human felicity is produced not so much by great pieces of good fortune that seldom happen as by little advantages that occur every day.'

Happiness is a little. If you cannot be happy with a little, it is very unlikely you will be happy with a lot. Practise happiness first on a small scale and work your way up from there. 'A great obstacle to happiness is to anticipate too great a happiness,' wrote Fontenelle. Great expectations make for small compensations.

Happiness is a dare. Life is a risk! So too is happiness. Occasionally you have to take a gamble. There will be times, almost inevitably, when the gamble won't pay off; this is what makes happiness all the sweeter when you experience it.

Happiness is a time for fun. Fun, laughter, play, recreation and generally jollying around adds to the happiness of life. Life is a balancing act between duties, responsibilities, work, rest and play – each has its place in the grand scheme of your affairs. Rewarding yourself with time for fun fills you with all of the 'happiness fuel' you need to keep going.

Happiness is loyalty. To be happy it helps to be loyal – to your family, to your friends, to your values and, above all, to yourself. Be true to your own vision and the people who genuinely love you will be thrilled for you. Trying to find happiness by following other peoples' ideas of it is rarely fruitful. Be true to your own vision.

Happiness is shared. 'All whom joy would win, must share it – happiness was born a twin,' wrote Lord Byron. One of the most important lessons of life is the lesson that states, quite simply, that what you give is what you get. If personal happiness is one of your ultimate goals in life, then giving a portion of this happiness back to others has to be very high on your list if you are to succeed. Happiness is a gift for others.

At the Laughter Clinic we play with a rich selection of creative growth games based on the happiness theme. Each and every one of these aims to explore and enhance the relationship between health, humour and happiness.

HAPPINESS GAMES

The key to any exercise is to dress appropriately – in other words, be ready to have fun! The more fun you have, the more you will want to play these happy creative growth games; and the more you play, the better they – and you – get!

HAPPINESS IS . . .

Approximately 40,000 people were once asked, 'What are your main goals in life?' Over 38,000 listed 'happiness' or 'contentment' as one of their goals. The next question was, 'Can you define happiness?' Research discovered that only 1 per cent had ever sat down to work out what happiness meant for them!

Take time out to create your own Happiness Charter. Remember, the more you focus on happiness, the easier it is to find.

STRIKE IT HAPPY!

To get the right answers in life it is important to ask the right questions! I recommend that you ask yourself this question once a month (or more frequently, if you can handle it!): 'What can I be doing, right now, to enhance my happiness?' Take 20 minutes or so to answer this question afresh each time. Look at every area of your life – work, family, love, education, leisure and spiritual growth. Make all your new beginnings today – tomorrows never come!

HAPPY HOUR

There is an insect that lives in the heart of the Amazon that has a lifespan of 59 minutes. After I first heard about this insect I became, for a short time, obsessed with this thought: *If I were to live for just one hour, what would I do to make it a happy one?*

Thankfully, most of us have a lot more than an hour in which to discover our happiness.

If you were to give yourself one hour of happiness, what would you do? Be realistic – no jetting off to Bermuda (you wouldn't even get there in an hour)! The joy of the happy hour game is that it makes you stop putting happiness on hold. You can experience 'now' – not 'after', 'if', 'when' or 'then'. Happy hour also reinforces the notion that if you cannot be happy with a little you will find it difficult to be happy with a lot.

One word of warning: You will never 'find' the time for a happy hour; you must *make* the time.

HAPPY DAYS

Be wise, give yourself a Personal Happy Day (PHD) from time to time! Think back over the last month – how many days would you describe as personal happy days? Personal happy days are for putting everything you cherish and value first.

Planning a personal happy day can be almost as much fun as the day itself. What will you do, this month, for your first personal happy day?

HAPPY NEW YEAR!

Resolutions, fresh intentions, new affirmations and a hopeful air herald the start of each new year. Belief in a better, happier, more fulfilling life is born again. You don't have to wait for the eve of 1st January to start a Happy New Year; have a Happy New Year party – or a Happy New *You* Party – tonight!

HAPPY BREATHING II

This is a creative relaxation exercise that builds on the *Happy Breathing I* exercise in Chapter 2.

Allow yourself to be physically comfortable and mentally calm, and then begin to deepen your breathing with every breath you take. Whenever your mind wanders, bring it back to the breathing and continue to breathe more and more fully and freely. Then, using your creative imagination, on the next exhalation imagine you are first breathing out an air of happiness; as you inhale, imagine you are breathing in happiness. Let your imagination take full flight! Breathe out happiness; breathe in happiness. Do this again and again until you feel you are calm and have done enough.

HAPPY FAMILIES

Question time again! What can we do, as a family, to help each other to be happy? Simple! The key is, of course, communication. Making time for family forums in which questions can be aired and shared can be such a rewarding experience. It's fun, enriching, easy to do and ultimately can help to bring a family closer together. Do we laugh enough? Do we play enough? Do we make enough time for fun? Don't just hope for it: go for it.

THE GIFT OF HAPPINESS

'Those who bring sunshine to the lives of others cannot keep it from themselves,' wrote James M. Barrie. At the Laughter Clinic we recognize that there is a severe shortage of genuine happiness in the world. Anything we can donate to the World-wide Fund for Happiness is a precious contribution to the happiness of us all.

How will you spread a little happiness today? What action will you donate, today, to the World-wide Fund for Happiness?

4

LAUGHTER AND SOCIETY

Good humour is one of the best articles of dress one can wear in society.
William Makepeace Thackeray

Most human beings will admit to almost anything, such as reading on the lavatory, talking to themselves when alone, carrying no handkerchief and buying country-and-western records; many are also quite happy to admit to having false teeth, implants, a bad temper or an overdraft. There is one thing, however, no one will ever, ever admit to: having no sense of humour.

'ANTHROPOLOJESTS'

Whoever decided to laugh first has, in my opinion, an awful lot to answer for!
Anonymous Anthropolojest

If the study of *physical* experiences of laughter is mostly the domain of medicine, and the study of *emotional* experiences of laughter is the focus of psychology, then the study of *social* experiences of laughter largely belongs to anthropology. Anthropolojests, as I shall affectionately call them, can be said to study the 'science of humour in man'.

Over the centuries, this study has unearthed some

fascinating facts, figures and theories about happy human behaviour. The anthropolojest will describe laughter as an evolutionary experience. Humour studies of both so-called 'primitive' and 'civilized' societies highlight laughter as an essential multi-purpose tool for growth, development, bonding and community-building. On one level laughter is a basic survival instinct, which can lend a new slant to the old phrase, 'He who laughs, lasts'. On another level, laughter is a bonding behaviour. On a higher level still, the anthropolojest views laughter as a human liberator. Indeed, there is a theory that proposes laughter, of all things, may hold the potential for finally liberating the human race as a whole from division, suffering, unrest and quarrel.

Origins of Laughter

'Mummy, who laughed first?'
'Keep quiet,' *Mummy explained.*
A real life incident!

The first and most important point anthropolojests consider is: where does laughter come from?

This simple question has no simple answer! Indeed, almost any 'simple' question about laughter ends either in mystery, paradox, uncertainty or yet another question. As one anthropolojest quipped, 'When it comes to laughter, before I've even begun, I already feel funny, slightly dizzy and at my wit's end.'

So, where do anthropolojests *think* laughter may come from? There are two main schools of thought.

UNIQUELY HUMAN?

One school of anthropolojests is prepared to bet that laughter is unique to the human species; they believe that no other creature has a capacity for humour. These anthropolojests then have to decide whether laughter is completely innate or learned. If laughter is learned, whom do we learn it from? Studies do show that children often develop a similar laugh and sense of humour to that of a particular parent. But what about 'in the beginning'?! From whom did the first person learn to laugh? Or did somebody laugh by accident one day?

If laughter is innate, from whereabouts does it spring? Some early anthropolojests played with the idea that there might be a laughter organ somewhere near the heart. Next came the search for a laughter gland. For a while it was believed the hypothalamus gland might have been hiding something from scientists. When the number of actual organs and glands was finally established, however, the search began to find a laughter chemical.

Some scientists even toyed with the idea of a possible laughter gene. The search for a 'laugh centre' in the brain has also proved fruitless. It is now recognized that laughter is an elaborate 'all-over-the-brain' experience.

EVOLUTIONARY?

The second school of anthropolojests believe that laughter is not at all unique to human beings and, indeed, that we may have inherited laughter from our evolutionary ancestors, the apes! In his classic work *The Expression of Emotions in Man and Animals*, Charles Darwin postulated that the action of laughter is descended from the 'baring of teeth' of apes. The idea is that when apes 'bare teeth' they ward off threats and that, similarly, when humans smile and laugh this sublimates aggression and communicates control. The 'ha ha' of humans is also occasionally linked to the 'wo wo' of apes!

I certainly like the idea of this school of thought. I feel sure that humans don't have exclusive rights to laughter. Many forms of life like to play, so it is quite natural to me that many forms of life may also like to laugh. Maybe the answer is that, just as humans have different laughs, creatures do too. Dogs, for instance, laugh with their tails; cats look like they smile, and maybe laughter to cats is a type of purr; dolphins play, smile and sound like they laugh; rabbits may laugh with their ears; and elephants play with their trunks! It is also my experience that, like play, laughter can happen across species The point is, we all laugh a little differently – that is part of the fun of it all.

The question remains: where does laughter come from? The answer is elusive, probably too simple to see. Some anthropolojests describe laughter as a divine gift sent to humans from the gods to make life on earth more tolerable. There is, unfortunately, no practical way of measuring the validity of this idea. Anyway, even if we could ask the gods where laughter comes from, they'd probably just laugh.

Defining Laughter

A laugh is a laugh is a laugh.

Inspired by Gertrude Stein!

Even the apparently simple task of defining laughter is enough to reduce anthropolojests (as it does psychologists) to tears. The more a 'laughologist' (to coin a phrase) studies laughter, the more impossible it is to define the thing. Quite simply, laughter defies definition.

Defining laughter would be much easier if there were not quite so many *causes* of it. We laugh so much, so often and in response to so many different things. For example, we may laugh in response to incongruity, surprise, triumph or a happy outcome. To complicate matters, we also sometimes laugh when we are sad, anxious, on the brink of defeat, suffering hardship, tired or confused. All things, some of the time, in some places, to some people, when the conditions are right, are laughable!

Anthropolojests prefer to study predictable human behaviours; laughter is totally unpredictable. The laughologist is tempted to think, from time to time, 'If only humans would co-operate by agreeing to laugh at a selected list of officially laughable things.' With a little bit of discipline like this we might be able to define laughter. Each human is a little different from all others, and laughter is, therefore, a unique experience we all share in common.

Defining laughter would also be easier if it didn't operate on so many levels. Laughter, as induced by tickling, is a purely physical experience. The 'all-over-experience' of laughter, on the other hand, cannot be confined to any particular part on the body. On some occasions, laughter is an emotional expression and release; at other times, laughter manifests as a social phenomenon. And then there are the spiritual theories, which aim to define laughter, and joy in particular, as expressions of the soul.

Laughter Epidemics

Laughter is a highly addictive positive contagion: if somebody starts, it's very difficult to stop.

R. Holden

Anthropolojests acknowledge that wherever there is a community there is also comedy. No anthropolojest has ever discovered a culture where laughter has been completely absent. Individual cultures and communities do exhibit different degrees of respect for and appreciation of laughter. However, it is safe and right to surmise that where there is life, there is laughter.

Not so long ago, the British culture attempted a dangerous experiment that aimed to do away with laughter. Fortunately this clumsy, half-witted experiment failed miserably. In Victorian times, a social disease commonly referred to as 'puritan ethic' reached its height, wiping out joy, laughter, fun, pleasure and humour in many households. With this disease, which was highly contagious and reached epidemic proportions, laughter became a madness, fun a sin, and play the devil's work. The Victorians considered laughter coarse, crude and uncivilized behaviour. This attitude was reflected in the dictionaries of the time, one of which described laughter as 'the product of an immature mind'. Victorian family photographs are famous for their obvious absence of fun, warmth, laughter and, above all, love.

This puritan ethic very nearly killed the spirit of laughter in Victorian times. If it had succeeded – if this epidemic had continued unchecked – the existence of our creative, spontaneous human spirit would have been seriously threatened. Fortunately, however, it lost its momentum. The after-effects remain in the form of, for example, 'British reserve'. The constant struggle for a healthy balance between laughter and seriousness, joy and solemnity, play and work, spontaneity and restraint continues.

To add a twist to this study of culture and humour, anthropolojests have occasionally witnessed laughter used as a form of punishment. In medieval times, for example, criminals faced 'firing squads' armed with old cabbages, rotten tomatoes, words of ridicule, mocking laughter and smelly eggs. Likewise, Eskimo communities make a habit of laughing in derision whenever a criminal's name is mentioned in conversation. Many preliterate communities across the world have similar social customs.

Then there are cultures – some of them poverty-stricken and decaying – where laughter is always found to be overflowing. Indeed, curiously enough, many anthropolojests have often found that the less material wealth a person has, the more laughter he or she is apparently given.

One of the most astonishing medical reports ever published appeared in the *Central African Journal of Medicine* (vol. 9, 1963), written by A. H. Rankin and R. J. Philip and entitled 'Epidemic of Laughter in Bukoba District of Tanganyika'. The authors wrote an account of a delightful social phenomenon in which whole African villages would be infected *en masse* by highly contagious bouts of laughter. The laughter would occasionally reach such a point that work and schooling would have to be postponed until the merriment died down.

On one famous occasion, one or two pupils at a Catholic girls' school began to giggle. The giggling gathered apace and soon the whole class was merry. Teachers were tickled by this spontaneous, joyful outburst and joined in. Soon the whole school was swimming in a tide of laughter. Word spread to the village, and when mothers came to collect their children they too became dizzy with laughter and chuckles of delight. That evening, when the men returned home, they too were overwhelmed by the laughter epidemic – so much so that no one slept that night and no one went to work or school next day.

This laughter soon landed on the doorsteps of neighbouring villages and the contagion continued to spread across a number of local communities. For a full two weeks the laughter continued in fits and starts. Tears flowed. Many people were treated for exhaustion. Trying to stop laughing only started the laughter all over again. In all, over one thousand people were affected by this astonishing 'infection'. Many people have witnessed similar incidents in Africa that have lasted for several hours, even a couple of days, but this is the longest ever laughter epidemic on record.

LAUGHTER AND CHARACTER

Laugh, and I'll tell you who you are.
R. Holden

Laughter is a language. Each time we laugh we tell people a little bit about who we are, where we are, what we think. how we feel and why. Our laughter communicates our personality. The German poet Goethe put it very well when he commented, 'Men show their character in nothing more clearly than by what they think laughable.'

What was once private becomes public as soon as we laugh. Ralph Waldo Emerson warned us all, 'A human being should beware how he laughs, for then he shows all his faults.' This is particularly true of those people who choose to laugh *at* life as opposed to laughing *with* it. Laughing *at* is often defensive, derisory and divisive; laughing *with* helps us to be comfortable, to connect and to bond. Happy, confident people tend to laugh *with*; unhappy, unconfident people tend to resort to laughing *at*.

The person who does not laugh at all sets alarm bells ringing. Thomas Carlyle was adamant: 'The man who cannot laugh is not only fit for treasons, stratagems and spoils; but his whole life is already a treason and a stratagem.' Rather harsh, I fear! An absence of laughter can impair psychological growth, however, as well as personal development and emotional expression. Without laughter, life can be a long, laborious hike across time.

Then there is the person who laughs too much! 'No one is more profoundly sad than he who laughs too much,' wrote the humorous German author Jean Paul Richter. Too much laughter can sometimes communicate too little happiness. There is so much to read into laughter. Behind every laugh, there is a story being told.

Best of all, from a character-building point of view, is the ability to laugh at oneself. The person who is happy to poke fun at his or her own victories and mishaps gains the respect of us all. To be able to laugh at oneself indicates a healthy ego, confidence, imagination, strength and a high degree of inner comfort. It is easy to be comfortable with people who are comfortable with themselves.

Types of Laughter

She had a penetrating sort of laugh. Rather like a train going into a tunnel.

P. G. Wodehouse

Your laughter is a label, your smile is a signature, your humour is your own personal coat of arms. We all laugh differently. Types of laughter go with types of people. How would you describe your smile? What words best describe your laugh?

A healthy ability to laugh can help you express all your emotions, thoughts and feelings, mainly because laughter is, itself, so expressive. Your laugh has its own particular rhythm, pitch, pace, volume and duration that is absolutely unique to you. Like the call of a bird in the wild, your laugh is your own password, imprint and signal.

'Lip smilers' smile only with their lips. 'Cheesy grin' people smile with their teeth. 'Twinkle smilers' smile with their eyes and eyebrows. 'Sweet smilers' exercise their chubby cheeks. 'Wry smilers' know something you don't. 'Tee-hee smilers' smile with their necks. 'Half-smile' people are only half with you. 'Body smilers' smile with whole heart and body. When you smile at somebody, how do you do it? And what does your smile say?

'Hearty laughter' is all heart. 'Belly laughter' is body, belly and heart. 'Seal laughter' (a barking laugh, like a seal's) sets people laughing. 'Laughing one's head off' can lead to headaches. 'Laughing up one's sleeve' suggests there's a secret somewhere. 'Horse laughs' set people racing. 'Bursts of laughter' create spontaneous pockets of sunshine. There are also giggles, chortles, chuckles, hoots, cackles, sniggers and guffaws. Laughter is, truly, a complex language.

LAUGHTER AND RELATIONSHIPS

Laughter is not at all a bad beginning for a friendship, and it is by far the best ending for one.
Oscar Wilde

Laughter is one of the essential lubricants that allows lasting relationships to run and run. Through laughter we learn to live and love happily. Many friendships are forged through laughter and preserved by laughter.

Friendships are often first born of moments of fun and laughter. For a stranger or an acquaintance to be promoted to the position of friend, that person must satisfy certain specific, though usually unconscious, criteria. One criteria will be humour. We judge a person partly by his or her laugh. As the great Russian novelist Fyodor Dostoyevsky once wrote, 'One can know a man from his laugh, and if you like a man's laugh before you know anything of him, you may confidently say that he is a good man.'

A well-appreciated sense of humour or one similar to your own is another important criteria for friendship. If two people cannot share laughter together it will be highly unlikely they will be able to share anything else. 'A difference of taste in jokes is a great strain on the affections,' wrote George Eliot. Friendships need fun for fuel.

In a fascinating research study published in *Psychology Today* (January 1979) entitled 'Different Jokes for Different Folks', James Hassett and John Houlihan collated and presented the findings of 14,500 humour questionnaires. Their final conclusion makes interesting reading. They wrote:

> *We expect our neighbors to disagree with our politics, our religion, our sex, and our opinion on the best quarterback in the NFL, but, for some mysterious reason, we expect people to share our taste in humour. If I love Monty Python or Saturday Night Live I'll fail to understand why someone else doesn't. If my favourite joke is greeted with a yawn, I'll fall back on excuses: 'I guess you had to be there.' Or else, 'Of course, I don't tell jokes very well' . . . The next time your favourite joke fails, instead of questioning your delivery, take a moment to marvel at the mystery of what makes people laugh.*

Joking Relationships

One funny friend in life makes up for all the trouble, toil and strife.
R. Holden

The discovery of the special, ancient, across-the-world social phenomenon of 'joking relationships' took place at the turn of the twentieth century. The term describes the playful pattern of social behaviour between two people who are usually related to one another either by birth or, in particular, by marriage. Since its discovery the phenomenon has inspired anthropolojests, sociologists, historians and laughologists alike to investigate the powerful interplay of fun, laughter and friendship.

It seems that on the continents of Africa, the Americas, Asia, Oceania and Europe many ancient, preliterate cultures and close communities exhibited examples of joking relationships. It was considered a moral duty and social obligation for the two parties of the joking relationship to ensure there was always a constant supply of laughter, joking and horseplay. Each person was granted a special licence to be cheeky and playful. Most of the exchanges between the two joking relatives, particularly in public, had to be high-spirited. The one overriding rule was, no offence should ever be taken. Failure to participate in this playful obligation was considered most shameful.

Joking relationships are also a common occurrence in modern societies all over the world, but they are now played out in less formal and less structured ways. The joking relationship of modern times can exist between any two people of any family. The two parties often operate rather like a comedy double act: one initiating the humour, the other acting as a perfect foil for the fun. Occasionally they may compete, joyfully, for title of best humorist. Each will appreciate the other's role, and once again, however saucy the humour becomes, no offence is ever intended or taken.

Everyone should have a joking relationship. To have one friend in life who you know is guaranteed to help you laugh is a wonderful blessing. It is good to share moments of fun with friends who fill you with joy; it is also good to be able to call on these special people when times are hard and when you desperately need to raise a smile. The sole aim of joking relationships is laughter for its own sake.

Happy Families

A good laugh is sunshine in a house.
William Makepeace Thackeray

It is often said that the family that eats together, keeps together. Extending this idea a little, I like to believe that the family that plays together, stays together, and also that the family that finds it easy to laugh together will find it easier to live together.

Laughter can carry a family through times of happiness and hardship, victory and defeat, delight and despair, agreement and discord. Laughter promotes love and belonging.

Laughter is as important to children as any vital vitamin or mineral. If the light of laughter is not allowed to glow, the children of the house will not be able to grow. Rod A. Martin, Ph.D. tells us in his article 'Using Humour to Cope with the Daily Stresses of Growing Up' (*Journal of Children in Contemporary Society*, vol. 20, 1988, pp. 135–54):

A healthy sense of humour may be an important element in the child's coping repertoire for dealing effectively with the stresses of childhood. The experience of mastery through humour learned in the crucible of childhood will also serve the individual well in later adult years.

Laughter is also very important for the adults of the family. Indeed, laughter is often one of the things that brings a couple together and keeps them together. And it is the adults' example that will encourage the youngsters to embrace the spirit of laughter throughout their lives.

Courting Laughter

What magic there is in a girl's smile. It is the raisin which, dropped in the yeast of male complacency, induces fermentation.

P. G. Wodehouse

Comedy often plays Cupid's Arrow. First impressions count and, according to interpersonal communication research, three of the most essential (and sensual) features a potential Romeo or Juliet first looks for are a pleasant smile, good humour and a happy laugh. Generally speaking men, in particular, respond to a smile; women, in particular, enjoy someone with a good sense of humour; and both men and women like to share laughter.

Laughter, as a mating call, communicates vital information that both Romeo and Juliet need in order to make the correct and proper next move. Most of these next moves are based on instinctive, intuitive and unconscious decision-making processes. Many lightning-quick assumptions, formulations and deductions are made and much of the initial input data on which these dating-decisions are based comes from smiles, sense of humour and laughter. A smile, sense of humour and laughter speak volumes about the Romeo or the Juliet who is standing before you. Is the smile natural? Is the laughter manipulative? The quality of the smile and the laugh will tell you if your Romeo or Juliet is the genuine article. Indeed, a single laugh or smile is often enough to deduce whether or not, for instance, Romeo is confident, Juliet is interested, Romeo is an ego-maniac, Juliet falls for ego-maniacs, Romeo wears Bermuda boxer shorts, Juliet is drunk, Romeo is a bit gauche, Juliet doesn't mind, etc.

Humour surveys find that, in general, a Romeo will try harder than a Juliet to be funny. If Juliet 'steps out of line' and starts to crack a couple of good one-liners, Romeo may well wither, for humour in a Juliet tends to indicate confidence, wisdom, intelligence and a well-developed personality – and a good 90 per cent of Romeos are not looking for these fine qualities on a first date! 'Nothing spoils a romance so much as a sense of humour in the woman – or the want of it in a man,' said Oscar Wilde.

Research shows that Romeos often like to open with a joke. Good humour increases Romeo's chances of a date with an appreciative Juliet. For instance, 'I don't dance, but I'd love to hold you while you do' may well work better than 'Hello Babe, do ya want a cup of coffee at my place?' W. C. Fields' line, 'My heart is a bargain today, will you take it?' may well work better than, 'Hi, I'm Mick Jagger's bodyguard.' There are, of course, exceptions to the rules, and this is, I suppose, what makes romance so complex and so rich.

Sexual jokes are the most preferred category of jokes for both men and women. The overriding reason for this preference has to do with nerves. Courtship, flirtation, the first date, the first kiss, proposals, engagements, weddings, wedding nights and honeymoons are among the most important events of our lives; laughter can help relax the nerves, soothe the stomach and release the flutters of the heart.

Comedians make much of the comedy of courtship. Humour can bring people together; it can also, however, offer happy consolation. A famous actress once said, 'The important thing in acting is to be able to laugh and cry. If I have to cry, I think of my sex life. If I have to laugh, I think of my sex life.'

Love and Laughter

Laughter is the shortest distance between two people.
Victor Borge

The absence of humour from a relationship is often a reliable sign that something, somewhere, is seriously wrong. By contrast, a happy supply of humour can help keep a relationship healthy, creative and strong. It is so much easier for two people to share love if they can also share laughter. Laughter allows us to love.

Through laughter we can learn to express all of our feelings. If a person finds it hard to laugh, he may well, for instance, find it hard to cry. Laughter is a 'let-go experience' which teaches us to trust in our feelings and make contact again with our natural, unrestrained Self.

By helping us to achieve happiness, completeness and

cohesion on the inside, laughter helps us to achieve these things on the outside, with others. 'Shared laughter creates a bond of friendship,' wrote W. Grant Lee, 'When people laugh together, they cease to be young and old, masters and pupils, worker and driver. They have become a single group of human beings enjoying their existence together.'

The real importance of laughter is as a symbol – a symbol of free, spontaneous, creative and peaceful living. At the instant of laughter we are on top of the world, together. And as the laugh falls away and we gather ourselves once more, we are relaxed, happy and peaceful, together. While the warmth of laughter is still alive, we catch a glimpse of how it is all really meant to be.

LAUGHTER REVELATIONS

1 Laughter is loving. We can learn to love through laughter. Like love, laughter is fun, celebration and togetherness. To keep laughing can help us to keep loving.

2 Laughter is freedom. Through laughter we can bring all our emotions into play. Expressing ourselves through laughter can inspire us to express ourselves in other ways. Laughter liberates us.

3 Laughter is natural. Each time we truly laugh we are spontaneous, creative, free.

4 Laughter is accepting. No ifs, no oughts, no musts and no should-bes. When we are laughing we delight in non-perfect moments and in a non-ideal world. Through laughter we live life as it is, not as 'if only'.

5 Laughter is forgiveness. Resentment is hard, heavy and makes our bodies tight; with laughter, we travel swiftly and our hearts are light.

6 Laughter teaches tolerance. Laughter promotes patience

and helps us to see the bright side of things. Through
laughter we learn to tolerate ourselves, and others.

7   Laughter is a language. Laughter talks, laughter listens.
Laughter is the human touch. We contact one another
through laughter.

8   Laughter is play. Life is play, love is play and laughter
is play. All is play. To play your part well, there will be
times when you will need to frown and smile, weep and
sing, cry and laugh.

9   Laughter is belonging. No you, no me, no them and us.
No isolation, no division and no separation. Laughter
links us all together in experience, learning and fun.

10   Laughter is living. It is a celebration, a victory and a
success, for when we are laughing we are truly alive.

LAUGHTER PRESCRIPTIONS FOR LOVING RELATIONSHIPS

*By helping a person to laugh, you are helping that
person to live.*

R. Holden

Many of the creative workshops on offer at the Laughter
Clinic focus on the practical art of maintaining happy, loving
relationships. These workshops always inspire a positive,
lively and imaginative response. To give you a flavour of what
we get up to, I would say the top five workshops from the
'Relating Well' files are: '10 Ways to Improve Your Laughter-
Life,' 'An Alien's Guide to the Art of Happy Human
Relationships,' 'Creating a Happy Home,' 'Ha-Ha-Happy
Families' and 'Let's Laugh Together.'

The 'Relating Well' workshops provide people with space
and time to explore, create and play with a number of
imaginative, life-enhancing creative growth games. We often

begin with the most important relationship of all, our relationship with our Self. We then move on to explore all relationships, major and minor, far and wide, close and cosmic! The accent is not on problems but potential, in particular, the potential for creative, loving and joyful relationships.

The best laughter of all comes straight from the heart. One of the most important lessons of laughter is that we should not be afraid to live life straight from the heart.

GAMES FOR YOUR HEART

These creative growth games are designed for your enjoyment and enrichment. They are exercises for the heart – but there is no need to consult your doctor before embarking on this exercise programme. These games may initially be quite risky, but ultimately they are completely safe!

SMILE TRIAL

The Smile Trial puts the theory of laughter as a universal language to the test. The aim of the Smile Trial is: *Smile today, more than any other day; double the smiles that come your way.* Smiling, like many other behaviours, is highly infectious.

Pick a day and, from the moment you rise and shine, start smiling. Smile at anybody, everybody and anything! Begin with relatives, perhaps, and then move on to your neighbours, the bus driver, fellow commuters and work colleagues. Leave no one out.Some of the funniest, most enjoyable moments at the Laughter Clinic have been when we have shared how we got on with our Smile Trial. The merry memories of this day will last and last.

GREETINGS!

There is a social dis-ease particularly prevalent in some parts of the world which I call 'Not-so-Badder-Itis'! Most people, when asked 'How are you?' hide behind tired clichés such as 'Surviving,' 'Can't complain,' 'Not so bad' and 'Could be worse.' The sad thing is that people respond in these ways even when they feel happy! It is almost as if it is not polite to feel good.

How do you greet people? I'll never forget the time I was introduced to somebody who said, 'Hello, Robert, how are your bowels?' There are indeed a lot of ways to say hello! Ask yourself: 'How do I like to be greeted by people?' The greeting you like is the greeting you should then go out and give.

A HAPPY HOME

What do you do to create an air of happiness around your home? Invest another inspirational 20 minutes of your life and ask that creative brain of yours to deliver a selection of top-class methods of happy home improvements. This contemplative exercise is an alternative form of interior decoration!

Is the carpet too clean to walk on? Is the sofa too expensive to sit on? Is the china too delicate to eat off? Ask yourself: How can I make this home more relaxed and comfortable? How can I make this home more hospitable? In what ways can my home become more fun? Be daring – turn the TV off from time to time. Organize playtime. Create a library of fun activities. Designate one night a month or so as Entertainment Night. Make time for family games. Hold a Joke-of-the-Month contest. Have a Storytime evening. Live, and be creative.

'THREE WISHES'

Play 'The Genie Game'. This allows each person in a family, group or partnership three wishes over a certain designated period of time, i.e. a week, month or year. You can ask for three wishes from each of the other players and you must grant three wishes to each of the other players.

For example, you may feel so tired one evening that you can wish for someone to take your turn washing the dishes. Or you may wish for a bit more consideration today from someone. The key to this game is that you each take responsibility to be the best genie you can. You will find that the more positive you are to your playing partners, the more positive your playing partners will be to you.

TOTAL QUALITY MOMENTS

This exercise is probably the most popular of all the creative growth games at the Laughter Clinic.

Humans aspire to quality of life; all too often, however, we immerse ourselves in quantity, not quality. Life seems to get in the way of our happiness.

Spoil yourself! Indulge yourself in life for a while. Open yourself up unashamedly to the infinitely good deal going on around you. Prescribe for yourself a treat, a reward, a gift, a little luxury – whatever it takes to make a Total Quality Moment (or TQM).

Many of the creative workshops at the Laughter Clinic begin with a moment of sharing our most total quality moments of the week: a flower in bloom, a bath with luxurious oils, an evening meal with friends, a theatre outing, a walk in the park, a favourite magazine, something a child says, a sunset or a starlit night sky. The ideal time to take care of quality is today. Remember, happiness is not a destination, it is a way of travelling.

HUMOUR INVITES

'I love comedy. It's the only art form that's also a social grace,' said Paul Reiser. 'You meet a sculptor at a party, you can't say, "He's terrific, look what he can do with the potato salad." ' There is no doubt that comedy is one of the most highly-prized forms of social currency.

Send out the humour invites! Walk on the funny side of

the street! And make a point of occasionally looking at the world through comedy-coloured spectacles. Enrich your environment by including an element of humour in your life. And be yourself: you are innately funny and lovable just as you are!

THE KINDNESS VIRUS

'The best portion of a good man's life – His little, nameless unremembered acts of kindness and of love.' So wrote William Wordsworth. Acts of selfless consideration and unconditional kindness inspire and enhance healthy, happy, loving relationships. Many of the most cherished, treasured memories of life are moments of complete kindness.

The Kindness Virus game is inspired by the belief that kindness creates kindness. It is also inspired by the words of Goethe: 'Kindness is the golden chain by which society is bound together.'

To play the Kindness Virus, give a day of your life to the universal cause of kindness. Make opportunities to be kind, for the sake of kindness. Take joy in giving joy. Look for no reward, and you will get your reward. Indeed, play this game right, and I believe you will never want to recover from the Kindness Virus!

A HAPPY PHILOSOPHY

Laughter can inspire the poet in us. One of the most revealing creative growth games of the Laughter Clinic is to write a poem dedicated to human happiness. Once the poet in us is aroused, the philosopher will also begin to stir. You can pick any subject related to happiness, i.e. celebration, laughter, love, kindness or joy. Relax, and allow the words to flow through you, and I am convinced you will surprise yourself.

Leslie Gibson, creator of the Comedy Cart for Morton Plant Hospital, shares a little gem simply called *A Smile*.

A SMILE

A smile costs nothing, but gives much. It enriches those who give it. It takes but a moment, but the memory of it sometimes lasts forever.

None is so rich or mighty that he can get along without it, and none is so poor but that he cannot be made richer by it.

A smile creates happiness in the home, promotes good will in business and is the cornerstone of friendship.

It can perk up the weary, bring cheer to the discouraged, sunshine to the sad, and is nature's best antidote for trouble.

Yet it cannot be bought, begged, borrowed or stolen, for it is something that is of no value to anyone until it is given away.

When people are too tired to give you a smile, give them one of yours. No one needs a smile so much as he who has none to give.

5

'SMILE MANAGEMENT' AT WORK

A laugh is worth a hundred groans in any market.
Charles Lamb

Smile Management is an innovative, empowering principle-led management philosophy that recognizes that in the often over-serious, unimaginative world of work, comedy is capital, humour is a big-business asset, fun and play can promote profit, mirth is a potential motivator and laughter (when appropriate) is a universal currency.

Taking Smile Management into the workplace can be rewarding, valuable and enriching for companies, directors, employees and customers and clients. 'Enjoyment in Employment' is an essential prerequisite for creative growth, innovative development and happy enterprise. Smile Management is a lot of fun, but it is no joke: it is a serious proposition inspired by four of the most important principles of business excellence:

1 The primary human resources of creativity, invention, vision, communication, effort and determination are the principal assets of any place of work. High-flying management techniques and clever corporate strategies, good as they may be, will always be inadequate if they forget to put human assets first.
2 Work is a glorious 'GO' – Goldmine of Opportunity for creative growth, self-discovery and personal development.

Work offers daily opportunities for learning new skills, enjoying social interaction, achieving goals, fulfilling a purpose, tasting success, learning from failure, building self-esteem and experiencing happiness. 'Happiness, I have discovered, is nearly always a rebound from hard work,' wrote David Grayson. There is no need to stop living to start work.

3   Work is a form of play. With a little imagination, work can be made to be a fun, full-hearted and personally fulfilling tonic. Many of the truly great business entrepreneurs have been fuelled by an effervescent spirit of fun, excitement and creative play.

4   Happy people produce happy results. In other words, making it fun can be a profitable formula for business success. Fun inspires creativity, innovation and ideas; happiness supports self-esteem and personal competence; laughter and smiles can boost morale and enhance team spirit; and a spirit of play will inspire energy, determination and achievement.

Alas, many managers are currently failing in their primary duty to create a happy environment conducive to the healthy growth of vital human resources. All too often, genuine praise, work satisfaction and even basic human decency are sacrificed as being 'nice, but non-profitable'. As a result, industrial diseases such as stress, communication breakdown, low morale, idea-droughts, absenteeism, high turnover and poor productivity proliferate.

If no attempt is made to make the workplace pleasant, what's the point? 'The brain is a wonderful organ. It starts working the moment you get up in the morning, and does not stop until you get into the office,' wrote Robert Frost. Unfortunately, this is what happens when vital human resources are neglected, undervalued, untapped and overlooked.

Much depends on attitude. Douglas McGregor outlined two opposing attitudes to work called 'Theory X and Theory Y' in his book *The Human Side of Enterprise*. Theory X-attitudes lead to the following sorts of assumptions:

- work is undesirable and disagreeable;
- money is the only motivation for work;
- workers want to get away with as little as possible;
- workers see responsibility as a burden;
- creativity is exclusive to management and
- workers need to be marshalled, manipulated and forcibly led.

By contrast, Theory Y-attitudes lead to the following sorts of assumptions:
- work can be interesting and rewarding;
- a sense of purpose, fulfilment and personal growth are obvious motivations for work;
- workers actively seek experience, training and new skills;
- workers respond well to being given personal responsibility;
- everybody has creative potential and an opinion well worth listening to; and
- the more you treat a worker well, the more a worker will want to work well.

Smile Management is a Theory-Y management philosophy which believes work can be for pleasure and not just pain. Social psychology surveys identify that work is potentially a very valuable source of happiness for both men and women. These surveys also identify that job dissatisfaction is for many people the major cause of personal unhappiness in life.

BENEFITS OF SMILE MANAGEMENT

*When work is a pleasure, life is a joy! When work is a duty,
life is slavery.*
Maxim Gorky

Every possible effort should be made to ensure work is enjoyable and rewarding. A highly-valued, well-motivated, happy workforce makes a lot of economic sense. Basically put, Smile Management can, both directly and indirectly, help to balance the books and boost the bottom line.

More and more companies, big and small, are starting to entertain the idea of humour programmes for the workplace. They realize that caring for the health, happiness and welfare of its employees can actually be cost-effective. The 'I Care/You Matter/This Job Should Be Fun' companies, as business consultant Bob Basso calls them, are not only highly pleasurable to work for, they are also highly profitable.

An increasing number of business humour initiatives are now being set up. They come in many different shapes and arrangements. More and more training programmes, in particular, are experimenting with interesting sounding workshops such as 'The Joy of Stress,' 'Team Spirit,' 'The Time of your Life' and, of course, 'Smile Management.' Other humour initiatives include juggling for executives, stress buster days, fun committees, orienteering adventures and comedy clubs.

Laughter in the workplace is essential but not all-powerful. For example, no amount of laughter can of itself transform a lousy book-keeper into a good accountant, and a happy smile, no matter how charming, will not be enough on its own to explain to your boss why you deserve a promotion this year. The key overall benefit of a humour initiative is that, humour helps make hard work easier. A few more essential benefits are listed below.

Happy Creativity

Joel Goodman of the Humor Project likes to explore with business people the intimate relationship between the *'Aha'* of creativity and the *'Ha-Ha'* of laughter. 'Humour and creativity are at least kissing cousins,' he explains. An appetite for fun and a capacity for creativity often go hand in hand.

Humour resources can inspire the human resources of imagination, invention, innovation and ideas. Medical research is able to demonstrate quite clearly that laughter can stimulate the right side of the brain, which is responsible for creativity, lateral thinking, the production of ideas and creative 'what if' explorations.

Problem-solving, decision-making, fear-free work environments and creative think-tanks are just a few of the tangible benefits that can accrue whenever and wherever creativity and fun are allowed full rein.

Stress Busting

Companies pay heavily for an absence of mirth in the workplace, because this is a tell-tale sign of too much negative stress. An absence of humour also leaves an individual and team much more prone to further outbreaks of negative stress. A healthy supply of humour can, on the other hand, create a climate in which negative stress is confronted, communicated and duly jettisoned.

The psychology of humour recognizes laughter as a natural, powerful stress buster that can help a person to release tension, gain a perspective and think more positively. In the workplace humour can be used to build up the happy triangle of happy thinking, happy people and happy results.

Team Spirit

No work team can function fully without humour. A free exchange of laughter between team members enriches each person's work output, willingness to co-operate, loyalty, appetite for hard work, ability to communicate freely, and overall sense of team spirit.

Motivation and Morale

Which would you rather try to motivate: a dead donkey or a happy puppy? Fun makes happy puppies of us all! Fun can be, at one and the same time, an aim of work, a product of work, a reward of work and an excellent motivator to work.

Communication

One of the most important rules of speech-making is 'make 'em listen: make 'em laugh'. Humour stimulates a listener's interest, attention-span, memory and receptivity. Humour also helps to hurry the time along! Approximately only 15 per cent of company employees read their company reports, the main reason being that most company reports are dry, dull and distinctly unimaginative. Memos, faxes, telephone messages, goal sheets and meeting minutes that are presented humorously, imaginatively or with creativity aforethought tend to give pleasure, make a point and inspire a productive, positive response.

Happy Working Relationships

Happy, rewarding results at work are often a product of happy, rewarding working relationships. Humour consultant Malcolm Kushner recommends in his book *The Light Touch*:

Just ask yourself these questions: Do you know someone who lacks a sense of humour? How do you feel about this person? Do you try to minimize your interactions with him or her? Do you try to avoid doing business with this person? Your answers should suggest why humour can play such an important role in establishing business relationships.

Productivity

Zig Ziglar, America's Number 1 Motivator, spells it out loud and clear in his marvellous book *Top Performance*. 'To ask a person to continue performing tasks he does not enjoy, is not committed to, and fails to perform satisfactorily dooms the individual to unhappiness and decreased productivity.' The most productive workforce in the world is a healthy, happy workforce led by a healthy, happy 'I-can-hear-you' management team. Enjoyment energizes employees; fun keeps us fighting fit; and mirth makes for merry motivation and morale.

Better Health/Less Absenteeism

Matt Weinstein, a humour consultant based in Berkeley, California, lectures to companies on the tangible link between over-seriousness and serious ill health. His own company motto is 'If you take yourself too seriously, there's an excellent chance you may end up seriously ill.' Conversely, work can be a wonderful medicine. I like to believe this is what Galen had in mind when he said, 'Employment is nature's physician, and is essential to human happiness.'

Quality Control

Happy people are not lazy, they are energetic and productive; happy people do not cut corners, they thrive on job satisfaction which is, itself, a result of high-quality performance. Bob Basso and Judi Klosek paint a portrait of a new, modern type of manager (called the Light Manager) in their book *This Job Should Be Fun*. They assert that one of the chief qualifications for being a Light Manager is 'to realize that the only way to improve quality is to allow people to enjoy their work, laugh, celebrate, and feel good.'

Mirth is a Marketing Tool

A winning smile makes winners of us all.

Anonymous

A smile is one of the most powerful selling agents in the world. The next time you sit before your television set, count the number of advertisements that use humour, laughter and smiles to get your attention, stimulate positive interest and help you to make up your mind! Companies often also employ comical logos, happy symbols and fun product-packaging to help promote their wares.

SMILE MANAGEMENT TIPS

Below you will find lots of tips for making the workplace a nicer place to spend one third of your life. Not all of the suggestions will work for you and your job, but they may help bring to mind possibilities for making your worklife more wonderful.

TOO MUCH LIKE HARD WORK? – STRATEGIES FOR JOB SATISFACTION

Far and away the best prize that life offers is the chance to work hard at work worth doing.

Theodore Roosevelt

1 Be full-hearted in your work. Be creative, allow your

imagination full rein and give it your whole heart. High-level performances are born of high-level commitment. What you give is what you get. 'Do your work with your whole heart and you will succeed – there is so little competition!' wrote Elbert Hubbard.

2 Keep your work fun and you will keep yourself fresh. 'Work is much more fun than fun,' said Noel Coward. Fun is a state of mind; for things to be fun, you must make the first move. Always ask yourself, 'What can I do to make this more fun?' When the fun flows so too does energy, enlightenment and enterprise.

3 Enjoy it. Do you know why you go to work? The first answer is usually money! What comes next? The more a person knows what he or she likes about work, the better he or she usually performs. 'We enjoy ourselves in our work – in our doing; and our best doing is our best enjoyment,' wrote Friedrich Jocobi. Stress surveys also show that people who have a keen sense of enjoyment at work tend to be healthier and more successful than those who turn up only for the money.

4 Be enthusiastic. 'The worst bankrupt is the person who has lost enthusiasm. Let one lose everything but enthusiasm and that person will again come through to success,' wrote H. W. Arnold. Carefully managed enthusiasm is a most splendid business resource that can inspire dedication, drive, originality and, above all, results. What is more, enthusiasm is highly contagious and can bring out the health, happiness and success in everyone.

5 Keep yourself amused. 'When men are rightly occupied, their amusement grows out of their work, as the colour-petals out of a fruitful flower,' wrote John Ruskin. Vary your work where possible; try to avoid boredom at all costs; test out new ways of thinking; keep exploring new options and keep acknowledging all the good stuff about

your work. The only way to keep ahead and to keep at it is to keep yourself amused.

6 Be encouraging. Give praise, be complimentary and be happy to acknowledge other people's successes. Friendly encouragement is as important to a person as fresh air. The psychologist William James believed that, 'The deepest principle in human nature is the craving to be appreciated.' Mark Twain put it another way when he said, 'I can live for two months on a good compliment.'

7 Get personal. Take a personal interest in all your business interests. Smile Management defines business as a 'people game'. All businesses, public and private, are basically people businesses. Show interest and make a solid connection with the people you work with and for. We all of us respond to a person who is prepared to take a genuine, sincere personal interest in our welfare.

8 Take pride and pleasure in your performance. No matter how small or apparently insignificant, work done well merits appreciation – yours as much as anyone else's. 'No race can prosper till it learns there is as much dignity in tilling a field as in writing a poem,' said Booker T. Washington.

THE 10-STEP HUMOUR PRODUCTION LINE

1 Fun Committees. The principal aim of a Fun Committee is to inject a spirit of fun into all parts of the workplace. A Fun Committee is made up of between four and eight democratically elected MDs (Mirth Directors) who are representative of the entire company structure. Any employee can forward suggestions to the MDs, who hold a Fun Committee meeting once a month or so. The very best ideas are then put forward to the management for serious consideration.

More and more companies are now exploring the positive benefits of Fun Committees, or MIME (Make It More Enjoyable) Groups as they are sometimes called. The ideas needn't be elaborate. Some typical ones include: a birthday party policy for company employees; Christmas parties and financial new year parties; a holiday photograph board; company memorabilia such as T-shirts, car stickers, badges and crazy mugs; colourful memos; and red-carpet treatment/celebrations when an employee has a baby: something like 'New Company Baby Day'.

2 Laughter Rooms. One of the chief functions of a Fun Committee can be to create a Laughter Room for employees to use during their lunch breaks and coffee breaks.

Step One: Circulate a questionnaire to all employees asking them what they would like to see in the Laughter Room.

Step Two: Place an order for funny videos, books, cartoon manuals, comedy cassettes and anything else that your budget can handle.

Step Three: Have a well-publicized opening day.

Step Four: Devise a video/cassette tape lending library scheme.

Step Five: Enjoy it!

A Laughter Room is one of the best refreshments available to a hard-working workforce.

3 'HAHA' Team. 'HAHA' stands for 'Honorary After Hours Activities'. A typical HAHA team organizes entertainments and other social opportunities for company employees and their families. Theatre trips, cinema visits, orchestra nights, 'Meal of the Month' evenings (going out for a company-sponsored feast), wine

and cheese evenings, company allotments, a company sports team – even a company holiday club can be initiatives inspired by HAHA teams. One of the benefits of a HAHA team is that it can offer cheap rates for outings by being able to group-book.

4 Save the Environment Squads. Productive workers need a productive environment and a productive environment requires constant creative and imaginative attention. The aim of the Save the Environment Squad is to ensure that the working environment always remains clean, pleasant and inspirational. Some of the chief considerations for this squad will include: lighting, colour schemes, office furniture, music, office fragrances, bulletin boards, pictures and posters, ionizers, temperature control, air conditioning, electromagnetic protection and VDU guidelines. Excellence is inspired by a happy environment.

5 Company Newsletter. A company newsletter is a wonderful tool for encouraging team spirit and motivation. The best company newsletters are created and designed in-house. Positive features may include employee profiles, a 'Good News' column, competitions, quizzes and crosswords, a classified advertising section, list of awards won by employees, progress updates and a promotions column. An imaginative public relations officer will also attract outside advertising and local special offers and opportunities for company employees.

6 Stress Buster Days. A fundamental aim of all company policies should be the reduction of all negative and unnecessary stress. A Stress Buster intervention may include relaxation workshops, on-site massage facilities, time-management seminars, team spirit-building exercises and other personal empowerment skills and events. Stress Buster days are as much about prevention as about cure – they can work wonders for a wobbly team spirit and low company morale.

7   Quality Circles. A quality circle is a worker-participation scheme that aims to devise and introduce methods for improving work quality, solving production problems, reorganizing workspaces, simplifying and improving work structures, communicating workers' needs, reviewing training requirements, enhancing communication systems and offering professional support to employees.

8   Job Enrichment. Too often, company managers are too busy talking at their employees to listen to them. One of the first steps of a job enrichment campaign is to ask the experts how their jobs could be improved, enriched and made even more productive. Some of the more enlightened job enrichment campaigns respect employees sufficiently to allow them to redesign their own jobs. Other considerations of job enrichment include flexi-time, job rotations, job share, frequent evaluations and various forms of employee consultation.

9   Company Celebrity of the Year. A company celebrity of the year event is a marvellous opportunity for colleagues, and their families, to relate to one another not as workhorses but as fully paid members of the human being club. The aim of the event is to discover the most talented entertainer-performer in the company ranks. Each nominee will demonstrate a cabaret skill such as singing, playing a musical instrument, performing comedy, magic or juggling, doing impressions or dancing. An elected panel of judges makes the final decision, with a little help from the audience! Company karaoke nights are similar: fun-filled and a talking point for months to come!

10 Fun(d) Raising. Working together for a common good is a marvellous way of exercising the team spirit muscle. Many teams get great joy out of raising funds or donating skills to a charity project or similar worthy cause. Another type of fund is the 'positive party' fund:

each time an employee is negative, late, loses something or lets slip an expletive, for instance, he or she donates a 'fine for a fine time' which goes towards a positive party evening for the whole staff.

15 STRATEGIES FOR LAUGHTER ON THE JOB

1 'Joke Walls'. Dedicate one wall of the building to jokes, cartoons, quips and funny sayings. The one abiding rule is that no joke can be X-rated! You can add appeal by offering a Joke-of-the-Month Award as selected by democratic vote. Jokes with special relevance to the company may also be particularly encouraged.

2 Comedy for Confidence. No book on humour would be complete without the words of the industrialist Joseph P. Kennedy, who once advised, 'Whenever you're sitting across from some important person, always picture him sitting there in a suit of long red underwear. That's the way I always operated in business. Comedy cuts serious business occasions down to size.'

3 The Company Mascot. Devise a competition among the workforce to create a company mascot. An award for the best idea always helps. A mascot adds to the identity of the company and encourages a sense of belonging. A mascot can also make good marketing sense.

4 Product Improvement Awards. A product or service improvement award is a positive worker-participation scheme in which the workforce is asked to volunteer ideas, innovations and recommendations for increased excellence and greater success. The workforce has an expertise that is all too often overlooked. Greater participation tends to promote greater productivity.

5 Smile Waves. Make a point of smiling and bidding 'Good

day' to as many of your colleagues as you see as soon as you enter the building. If you are sincere you will create a small 'smile wave' as your colleagues will feel suitably impressed to pass on a smile to others. Smiling first thing is the best way to ensure you are still smiling last thing.

6 Compliments. Make it a diligent practice to give away a sincere, unconditional compliment or good word from time to time. Make a point of making somebody's day, every day, with a simple, sincere compliment.

7 Monday Clubs. It can be good fun and highly beneficial to make one lunchtime a week a special event. A Monday Club aims to transform the 'Thank God it's Friday' feeling into 'Oh Good, it's Monday.' Monday Club lunchtimes may involve pizza parties, a trip to the local pub, Chinese takeaway or even some homemade cooking. Each week a different person should be designated organizer for the day and given a brief to come up with something different and enjoyable.

8 'Aloha Fridays'. Hawaii has found a unique way to have fun and boost productivity: the last day of the working week is crowned Aloha Friday. All of the workforce come to work dressed in casual, relaxed and colourful clothes. Companies testify again and again to a miraculous metamorphosis on this day among their workers and production levels.

9 Celebration Days. It is only natural to want to celebrate when we achieve. Enlightened companies encourage employees to celebrate and make a point of rewarding them handsomely whenever they reach their goals. A celebration day is a way of saying 'thank you,' 'well done' and 'I really value your efforts'. Enlightened companies understand that if they reward well they will be rewarded well.

10 A Financial New Year Party. This is the ideal opportunity to publish new targets, motivate workteams, praise good performances of the old financial new year, welcome new team players and raise a toast to future successes.

11 Bonus Day Awards. A Bonus Day Award is inspired by the idea that it's not how much you work that counts, but how well. A Bonus Day Award means that, whenever a workteam achieves a preset target ahead of schedule, they are rewarded with a bonus day or afternoon off. Everybody will work hard and work well in response to this idea!

12 Juggle for Joy Sessions. Add one professional juggler to a roomful of tired workers and you will be astonished at how quickly they are re-energized by laughter and enjoyment. Strange as it may sound, you will discover there are few things more genuinely satisfying in life than learning to juggle!

13 Creative Canteen Management. With a little imagination and some good management, the dull, dreary canteen can be beautified so that it appeals to everyone's appetite for food and enjoyment. Even the introduction of a good vending machine with plenty of options can have a noticeable impact on employees. Good cooking makes a good company!

14 A Games Room. More and more companies are happy to provide a games room for their workers. Many larger companies spare no expense in providing equipment, fitness gyms and exercise spaces for its employees. The smaller companies can still provide a snooker table, darts, table tennis, chess and cards, for instance. It should also be possible for most companies to organize discount group memberships at local gymnasiums and sports clubs.

15 'Gone Fishing' Day. A 'Gone Fishing' Day is an office
    outing. The place, event and theme of the day should
    be for everyone to decide. If a team is to work well
    together it is important that they are able to play well
    together.

6

THE ART OF LIVING JOYFULLY

*I am persuaded that every time a man smiles, but much
more when he laughs, it adds something to this fragment
of life.*

Laurence Sterne

Poets, priests and philosophers have since time immemorial
amused and bemused themselves with a study of laughter.
'Is laughter a sin?' they have pondered. 'Does God enjoy a
good joke?' 'Is the soul ticklish?' 'Is it possible to take
humour with you through the eye of the needle?' 'Will there
be "No Laughing" signs in heaven?' 'Does humour tarnish
halos, or make them shine brighter?'

We know laughter is good for your physical and
emotional heart, but what of the spiritual heart? Does
laughter have any positive spiritual significance to speak of?
Opinion is divided; but there does definitely exist a golden
thread of wisdom and spiritual teaching that asserts that
laughter can be a truly healthy, 'nothing-to-be-guilty-about'
experience of mind, body and soul. It will be OK to laugh
in heaven!

Humour can be heavenly in that we are uplifted and
renewed by the spiritual splendour of healthy, joyful
laughter. One of the chief functions of laughter is that it can
help to liberate, if only for a moment, the fear-free spirit of
unconditional joy that rests deep within the heart of each
and every one of us. The experience of laughing joyfully is

as an essential initiation that takes us closer and closer to the experience of living joyfully.

THE LAUGHING BUDDHA

It is a test of a good religion whether you can make a joke of it.

G. K. Chesterton

All of the great spiritual traditions of our world deliver, in their original form, a gospel of joy. Christians, Jews, Muslims, Hindus and Buddhists share in common that they all revere spiritual teachings that are rich in holy commandments of love, celebration, rejoicing and joy. On awaking one time from a meditation divine, the German mystic Jakob Boehme was moved to say, 'We are all strings in the concert of His [God's] Joy.'

Throughout history, the joys, warmth and laughter of spirituality have all too often been drowned out by the cold waters of separatist, over-serious, sanctimonious, suffering-to-be-spiritual religions. Consequently, in time the joyful, friendly, playful God became eclipsed by the man-made judgmental, fearful, punishing God. Ultimately, we were taught to believe that laughter and joy were no longer by design of the divine, but rather were the work of the devil.

The Christian Bible, rewritten and re-edited more times than any well-trained theologian cares to consider, retains numerous references to joy. In summing up his great teachings Jesus says (John 15: 11), 'These things have I spoken unto you, that my joy might remain in you, and that your joy might be complete.' The Bible speaks of the 'joy of thy Lord', of 'Joy [as] the fruit of the spirit' and heaven as 'a kingdom of joy'.

In Acts 13: 52 we read how 'the disciples were filled with

"joy" and with "the Holy Ghost." ' In the Luke 6: 21 there is given a divine promise of holy laughter: 'Blessed are ye that hunger now: for ye shall be filled. Blessed are ye that weep now: for ye shall laugh.' Through the centuries Catholics have worshipped the Seven Joys of the Virgin: the Annunciation, Visitation, Nativity, Epiphany, Finding the temple, Resurrection, and Ascension. Martin Luther, German Protestant leader and Bible translator once opined, 'If you're not allowed to laugh in Heaven, I don't want to go there.'

The Buddhist tradition is proud to uphold the legend of the Laughing Buddha, whose joy, laughter and enlightenment transcend all earthly pain, suffering and ignorance. The Buddhist holy scripture, the *Dhammapada*, encourages us all to radiate joy. In Chapter 15, verses 197–200, the wisdom of the ages beseeches us all,

O let us live in joy, in love amongst those who hate!
Among men who hate, let us live in love.

O let us live in joy, in health amongst those who are ill!
Among men who are ill, let us live in health.

O let us live in joy, in peace amongst those who struggle!
Among men who struggle, let us live in peace.

O let us live in joy, although having nothing! In joy let
us live like spirits of light!

Spirituality without the eternal fountains of laughter, fun and joy make for a barren heart and a dark soul. Quite simply, if enlightenment is not meant to be joyful, what is its purpose? Joy is the subtle fragrance of enlightenment, the essence of liberation and the manifestation of someone who is learning to function more fully.

Lao Tzu, the legendary philosopher of Taoism, recognized laughter as being essential to life: 'If there were no laughter, the Tao would not be what it is.'

The Hindus and Yogis of the East follow a particular path of Yoga called Bhakti Yoga, which roughly translated means, 'Union with God through love and joy.' The two holy works of Hinduism, the *Upanishads* and the *Bhagavad Gita*, are two very joyful expositions devoted to study of the nature, potential and unfolding of the human spirit. The Katha Upanishad teaches us that 'When a man has heard and has understood and, finding the essence, reaches the Inmost, then he finds joy in the Source of joy.' And in The Taittiriya Upanishad we are told 'Joy comes from God. Who could live and who could breathe if the joy of Brahman filled not the universe?'

The Bhagavad Gita is very direct: 'The Essence of our Being, our Self, is Joy, *Ananda*.' The word ananda often forms part of the blessed names given to spiritual disciples to remind them that 1) their essence is joy; 2) their mission is joy; 3) their service is joy and 4) their goal is joy. Paramahansa Yogananda (author of *Autobiography of a Yogi*) and Anandamayi Ma are two fine examples of ananda yogis who have made it a part of their purpose to spread a gospel of joy.

Anandamayi Ma once delivered a contemplation on laughter which highlights the rich connection between spirituality and joy. It reads:

Laugh as much as you can – it will release all the
contractions in your body,
Let your laughing come from the deepest part of your heart,
let it shake you from head to toe,
If your soul is asleep you will only laugh from your lips,
I want to see you laughing with your mouth – with your
heart – with all your life's breath.

To do this, try to bring about a harmonious connection
between your inner self and your outer self,
And with all the energy you have, dedicate yourself to God
alone
Then your laughing will pour forth joy everywhere.

A GOSPEL OF JOY

Let there be mirth on Heaven and Earth.
R. Holden

The words 'pleasure' and 'joy' traditionally define the two distinct types of happiness available to human beings: pleasure describes happiness attained through physical, emotional and material objects, pursuits and ends; joy describes the happiness that is found through spirituality and self-realization. Pleasure is momentary; 'joy' transcends all moments in time and lasts forever.

Unfolding our innate spiritual, creative potential is one of the highest tasks we can undertake. Joy is the goal; it is also the key. Spirituality without heart, without fun and without laughter is like a Heaven with no angels and an Earth with no sunlight. All of the great spiritual traditions offer us codes of conduct and ways of being that allow us to receive and radiate joy.

Philosophers have always been uncertain about the value of laughter on the path of spiritual unfoldment. Plato, Pythagoras, Kant and Descartes, for example, have not always been entirely complimentary. As the humorist H. L. Mencken so rightly points out, however, 'There is no record in human history of a happy philosopher'! The failure to look for and maximize the potential spiritual benefits of laughter is one important reason for the decline of organized religions; they are too dry and sterile to strike a spark in many people's hearts.

Deep within the great spiritual teachings of our world there has always lived a gospel of joy, which is only now being rediscovered and re-examined. This joyful gospel holds a permanent place in the spiritual disciplines of fun, humour and laughter.

A GOSPEL OF JOY

LAUGHTER IS A GIFT FROM GOD

'God is the creator of laughter that is good,' proclaimed Philo, the Jewish philosopher of the first century AD. Laughter that is good, positive and life-affirming has often been reverenced by poets, priests and philosophers as a sacred energy and blessing from God.

Traditional portraits of the Creator, have often painted a picture of a solemn and severe dictator, yet through the ages there have always been spiritual teachers who have considered laughter to be a divine gift that can lead to divine prosperity. 'God cannot be solemn, or he would not have blessed man with the incalculable gift of laughter,' wrote Sydney Harris.

Laughter has a spiritual value and purpose in that it provides an expression and experience of our total Self. All emotions have this spiritual value and purpose for, as the English poet Leigh Hunt once wrote, 'God made both tears and laughter and both for kind purposes; for as laughter enables mirth and surprise to breathe freely; so tears enable sorrow to vent itself patiently.' All emotions have a potentially positive spiritual purpose.

LAUGHTER IS AN EXPRESSION
OF THE SOUL

Sir George King, UNICEF peace-prize winner and founder of the spiritual task force called The Aetherius Society, once told an audience (in his speech 'I Will Walk with You' given in 1964), 'Happiness is laughter of the mind; Joy is laughter of the soul.' Here, once again, we see the close-knit relationship between joy, happiness, laughter and the soul.

Laughter allows us to make contact with the whole of ourselves – nothing is left out. During moments of laughter we experience what it is to be connected, unified and perfectly integrated – there are no barriers and no falsities. Laughter is soulful.

JOY IS OUR BIRTHRIGHT

The gospel of joy, as communicated through so many of our most enduring spiritual traditions, tells us that to be full of the light and life of laughter is our birthright. Joy is innate, a part of our essence and a part of our destiny. Alas, this birthright needs to be exercised if it is to be realized. 'One inch of joy surmounts of grief a span, because to laugh is proper to the man,' wrote the French philosopher, priest and physician François Rabelais.

JOY IS A HEALER

Joy can 1) release negative mental dis-eases such as anxiety, over-seriousness and anger; 2) invite the positive expression of tears, hope, optimism and love and 3) encourage the whole Self to work towards health, happiness and well-being.

A healthy use of laughter can offer us psychological and spiritual immunity against physical, emotional and mental disturbances. 'Joy, temperance and repose/Slam the door on the doctor's nose,' wrote the American poet, Henry Wadsworth Longfellow.

LAUGHTER IS A FORM OF PRAYER

There is an old saying that goes, 'Next to a good soul-stirring prayer is a good laugh, when it is promoted by what is pure in itself.' Laughter is a song of the soul, a merry religious lyric, a devotional hymn. Through laughter we can celebrate, give praise, spread love and demonstrate our thankfulness. Laughter is one more way of worshipping this miracle we call life.

LAUGHTER IS WISDOM

'Laugh if you are wise,' wrote the Latin poet Martial. So many of the great spiritual teachers of our world have had a marvellous appetite for fun, play and laughter. Laughter preserves and fortifies us; it can give us the strength and resolve to press on; it offers relief and respite when we are tired and weary; through laughter, we learn.

Self-realization without laughter, spiritual progress without joy, wisdom without wit – all seem empty and devoid of purpose and meaning. Laughter is natural to us; joy is our enlightened state. It is hard to believe that the treasures of enlightenment could not include the jewels of laughter and joy.

LAUGHTER IS LOVE

Thomas Carlyle once wrote, 'True humour springs not more from the head than from the heart, it is not contempt, its essence is love.' Laughter can facilitate love; love can facilitate laughter. To put it another way: through laughter, we learn to love; through love, we learn to laugh.

JOIE DE VIVRE

It is more fitting for a man to laugh at life than to lament over it.

Seneca

The people who demonstrate a true appetite for life tend to respect that the art of living joyfully is not an arbitrary affair;

rather, they see living joyfully as a skill that requires regular practice. Whatever you want to achieve in life, the number one rule is it takes work to make it work. (Sometimes this work means merely allowing something to happen.) Living joyfully is no exception.

Joie de vivre is all about being as fully alive as possible. The American writer Henry Miller once contemplated, 'The aim of life is to live, and to live means to be aware, joyously, drunkenly, serenely, divinely aware.' Through a spirit of *joie de vivre* we aim to open up to a world of all possibilities, a world in which we can play with, develop and express our true spiritual potential. Laughter is all part of the fun of this aim.

Joie de vivre is not a happy-go-lucky philosophy. Luck is a lie; good fortune, on the other hand, is real. The difference between luck and good fortune is that with luck we get something for nothing; with good fortune we *earn* what we get through all that we think, do and are. *Joie de vivre* is all about investment, dedication and courage of enterprise. It is a definite gamble and a total commitment – the goal is to be fully awake, fully realized and fully alive.

Our lives are often immeasurably enriched when touched by those people who walk in the world with a spirit of wonder, excitement and *joie de vivre*. They remind us of our own innate potential to grow and evolve in life through laughter and joy. Studying such people is an eminently worthwhile pursuit. On close inspection it is possible to identify certain traits these people share:

- Thankfulness. We start winning the prize of living as soon as we pay thanks and give praise for all that we already have. Wealth is an attitude that makes a daily practice of gratitude and thanksgiving. How happy we are depends much upon the depth of our gratitude and thankfulness. You will find that, the more thankful you are, the more there is to be thankful about. The simple act of thankfulness can enrich and change your life. 'Gratitude is heaven itself,' wrote William Blake.

- Zest. 'What hunger is in relation to food, zest is in relation to life,' wrote Bertrand Russell. People who live on *joie de vivre* practise a way of life that exercises all of their energy, effort and enterprise. These people work fully, play fully and rest fully. The *joie de vivre* philosophy is based on the practical theory that states to get the best, give the best – always, without exception.

- Action. In my book *Stress Busters* I make a distinction between anxiety-orientated people and action-orientated people. The number one rule of anxiety is that, 'Anxiety has never once in the whole history of the human race solved a problem.' The number one rule of action is that 'The universe only rewards action.' *Joie de vivre* inspires an action-orientated approach to life. (And sometimes this 'action' can be to do nothing at all!)

- Responsibility. You are honour-bound to assume full responsibility for all that you encounter and experience. One of the ultimate joys of *joie de vivre* is that you need look nowhere else for inspiration than within yourself.

- Enjoyment. The French writer Emile Zola once said he would like to pioneer a new religion with one commandment only: 'Enjoy thyself.' Those people who radiate *joie de vivre* are adept at enjoying themselves and at passing enjoyment on to others. They have, in particular, an endless appetite for fun, play and laughter.

- Celebration. To live each and every moment of your life as a celebration of life itself ignites the spirit of *joie de vivre* deep within your soul. Each moment is special; there are no insignificant spaces in life. *Joie de vivre* empowers you with the will, intensity of purpose and drive to vitalize every moment with love, laughter and joy.

- Vision. Purpose, meaning and direction are life-blood to the person with *joie de vivre*. 'This is the secret of joy,' wrote

Evelyn Underhill, 'We shall no longer strive for our own way; but commit ourselves, easily and simply, to God's way, acquiesce in his will and in so doing find our peace.'

• Reverence. All things in life are sacred to the person who has a deep inner love for life. The spirit of *joie de vivre* is born of the spiritual outlook, appreciation and understanding that drive a person to make contact and become one with the true essence of all things. 'Thou art all Laughter, I am a smile; We are One,' wrote Paramahansa Yogananda.

• Realization. *Joie de vivre* draws a person to experiences, lessons and initiations that support constant growth, renewal and fulfilment. *Joie de vivre* concerns itself not only with personal growth but with the growth of communities, civilizations and the world. Be guided through life by this simple statement: 'Is this world a happier, more enlightened place because of who I am and what I do?'

JOYFUL LIVING

Let us live while we live.
Philip Doddridge

Exploring and practising the art of joyful living is one of the central creative themes of the Laughter Clinic. Almost all of the creative growth games we play with are designed in some way to activate the 'organic batteries of joy' that rest deep within us. The Art of Joyful Living workshops are thoroughly practical, creatively challenging and therefore, for most people, among the most enjoyable workshops of all. A list of joyful living growth games begins below.

The starting point for any joy workshop is that joy is *not* a commodity; it is a quality. In other words, joy cannot be given or taken, bought or sold, donated or stolen. It is a quality of heart, an attitude of mind, a dimension of soul. No one can give you his joy; he can only encourage you to find your own. When it comes to creating your own joy, others can help but only you can do it. You have the power.

Being joyful, then, does not have to depend on: (a) finding exactly the right person who behaves in exactly the right way; (b) being in exactly the right place at exactly the right time or (c) having exactly the right things happen to you in exactly the way you wish for.

What goes on *around* you need not determine or dictate exactly what goes on *inside* you. This is one of the most important points about joyful living. The way we respond to life is our decision, not a forgone conclusion. We can, all of us, pull our own strings, at any time, if only very gently. A little courage and a little effort often inspires a big result.

Keep laughing – keep loving – keep living!

LIVING JOYFULLY GAMES

When you need help finding a way to live life with laughter, refer to the following string-pullers!

RISE AND SHINE!

The first few minutes when you wake up are the most precious of all, for they can establish a mood that lasts all day.

On rising, give yourself every possible opportunity to shine! Give yourself space, time and attention; be good and kind and considerate to yourself. Create a routine or a ritual that will enable you to live in splendour for the rest of the day. Happy beginnings have a habit of inspiring happy endings.

The yogi Paramahansa Yogananda gave the world a marvellous meditation entitled *Spreading Divine Joy.* It begins: 'Beginning with the early dawn each day, I will radiate joy to everyone I meet. I will be mental sunshine for all who cross my path. I will burn candles of smiles in the bosoms of the joyless. Before the unfading light of my cheer, darkness will take flight.' Allow yourself an enjoyable moment or two to create your own inspirational 'rise and shine' meditation.

TODAY!

Today is a once-in-a-lifetime opportunity. The past is done, the future awaits – the present is all we have.

Part of the art of joyful living is to capture, celebrate and make the most of the moment. Each and every day ask yourself, 'How can I celebrate the miracle of life?' Whatever you do today, try to make it a day you'll remember even 20 years from now. Make it one of the 'good old days'. Live – fully – one day at a time.

FOR THE FIRST TIME!

Each day is a debut for those who live anew.

Invest a day in your life to look, listen, taste, touch and smell as if for the very first time. Empower yourself with a spirit of adventure, an air of appreciation and a heart full of love and gratitude. Look at your loved ones as if for the first time; listen to a bird's song as if for the first time; taste your food, smell a fragrance, touch someone for the first time. Drink it all up; take it all in. There are no repeats. Take nothing for granted.

GIVE PRAISE!

Send forth your love, your joy and respect to the people you meet in your life. Always be sincere, always be generous. If your praise is unconditional you cannot ever incur bad debts. A compliment, kind words, a positive greeting, special recognition and a smile – these are the little things that make life so worth while. Pope John Paul II once said, 'There is no law which lays it down that you must smile! But you can make a gift of your smile; you can be the heaven of kindness.'

CONTENTEMPLATE!

Make space and time for con*tent*emplation – the Laughter Clinic's alternative to contemplation. A joyful work of prose, eternal words of poetry, a beautiful view, a flower, inspired art, works of spiritual radiance – each of these is an ideal, fun subject for contentemplation. Allow yourself to transcend 'everyday experiences' so as to attune yourself more fully to 'special-day experiences'. Contentemplations are creative moments of joy in which you can make contact with something bigger, something wiser, something universal.

BLESS IT!

Make everything you do, everything you have and everything you give a blessing. Bless your thoughts, your actions and your experiences with joy, with love and with laughter. Bless your moments of triumph; bless your moments of despair. Work with, not against, everything you have, and everything you have will work with you. Whatever it is, bless it, and you will be blessed also.

HARMONIZE!

Harmonize, integrate and become one with whatever you choose to do, wherever you choose to go, whomever you choose to be with. 'Let my love spread its laughter in all hearts, in every person belonging to every race. Let my love rest in the hearts of flowers, of animals, and of little specks of stardust,' wrote Paramahansa Yogananda. Sit still for a moment and become the object, person or feeling that is closest to you.

SERVE AN ACE!

Give yourself away today. Be of service to the world today. Donate your efforts to a cause today. Serve an ACE today– ACE is Laughter Clinic-lingo for Abundantly Charming Effort! People who live joyfully tend to live generously. They have worked it out for themselves that giving does not diminish them: it enriches them. The Aetherius Society founded by Sir George King has a wonderful mission statement: 'Service is the jewel in the rock of attainment.' When the motive is unconditional, the rewards are inspirational.

BE A SMILE MILLIONAIRE!

Or a 'joy billionaire', as Paramahansa Yogananda put it: 'I will try to be a joy billionaire, finding my wealth in the coin of Thy realm – ever new bliss. Thus I shall satisfy my need for spiritual and material prosperity at the same time.' Be rich, give generously and your personal wealth will multiply. Laughter, smiles and moments of joy are cherished treasures that finance life.

SOMETHING NEW!

'Each day the world is born anew/For him who takes it rightly,' wrote James Russell Lowell. Renew yourself each and every day. Make a point of exploring, experiencing or learning something new today. Live life as an adventure. Today you are reborn. Make the most of it!

LAUGHTER IS LIBERATING

When we laugh for joy we can transcend so much of what keeps us down, feeling low and under-par. Laughter liberates our creative resources; it lifts our spirits; it encourages freedom of expression; it keeps a check on the potentially over-serious ego; it lends perspective to pain; it allows us to play; it can also help us to rise above and leave behind personal limitations and suffering. Humour takes us up towards our higher Self.

DIRECTORY OF HAPPINESS AND HUMOUR RESOURCES

For further information about The Happiness Project and for details about 1) public workshops, 2) books and tapes, 3) the '8 Week Happiness Programme', 4) the 'TEACHING HAPPINESS' professional certificate training, and 5) the 'Deep & Meaningful Corporate Training Programme', contact:

The Happiness Project
Elms Court
Chapel Way
Botley
Oxford OX2 9LP
Tel: 01865 244414
Fax: 01865 248825
Email: hello@happiness.co.uk
Website: www.happiness.co.uk

USEFUL ADDRESSES

The following contacts include groups, centres and therapists who work with healing and happiness, healing and joy, healing and laughter.

UK

Leon Lawrence
Public Relations Officer
Clowns International
28 Denison Close
Ossulton Way
London N2 0JT
Tel/fax: 0181 444-8406

Val Rainbow and Sid Revill
34 Stratford Road
Shipston-on-Stour
Warks CV35 5AU
Tel: 01608 663480
Workshops for Play – healing, happiness and wholeness.

Clowning and Physical Theatre
The City Literary Institute
Stukeley Street
London WC2B 5LJ
Tel: 0171 430-0544

Ben Renshaw
PROteen
Suite 11
2 St Quintin Avenue

London W10 6NU
Tel: 0181 964-2624
Personal/social skills for young people, and workshops on '100% Happiness'.

Dr Barbara Cooper
(Dr Quackers)
31 Lowther Road
Eaton Rise
Norwich
Norfolk NR4 6QN
Tel: 01603 451435
Conventional/holistic doctor and clown.

The Smilenium Project
'Licence to Smile'
14 Brookfield Close
Mill Hill
London NW7 2DA
Tel: 0181 959-4983

Oddballs
200B Chalk Farm Road
Camden
London NW1 8AF
Tel: 0171 284-4488

134 LAUGHTER, THE BEST MEDICINE

Also Brighton – Tel: 01273
 696068
Juggling, kites, magic, rollerblades.

Robert Holden
The Happiness Project
Elms Court
Chapel Way, Botley
Oxford OX2 9LP
Tel: 01865 244414

L.I.F.E. Foundation
Mind, Body, Heart Technology
Maristowe House
Dover Street
Bilston
West Midlands WV14 6AL
Tel: 01902 409164
*Courses on laughter, joy, healing
and holistic health.*

Findhorn
Holistic Health Care
5 Bank Lane
Forres
Morayshire, Scotland
IV36 0NU
Tel: 01309 674911
Fax: 01309 691301
email: healthcare@findhorn.org

Didier Danthois
Sacred Clown as Healer
32 Rosemary Avenue
London N3 2QN
Tel: 0181 343-0255
*Performances for healing, joy and
spirituality.*

Carolyn Goodman
Spotted Cow Cottage

Albourne Road
Hurstpierpoint
Sussex BN6 9ET
Tel: 01273 833980
Healing Full Member of NFSH.

Jeannette Sloan
Agape House
Holistic Education Centre
16 Simpson Road
Walton Park
Milton Keynes MK7 7HN
Tel: 01908 201113
Fax: 01908 392203
*Workshops on 'A Pocket Guide to A
HAPPY LIFE'.*

Dee James
The Chiron Therapy Centre
Gentlemans Farm
Bardfield Saling
Essex CM7 5ED
Tel/fax: 01371 850414/851133
Email: chirontherapy@msn.com

Catherine Z. Mativi
SMaT Ltd
Stress Management Training
31 Gunhild Close
Cambridge CB1 4RD
Tel/fax: 01223 240335

Sue Boyd
MSc Health Promotion/R.G.N.
Prospect House
41 Church Road
Westbury-on-Trym
Bristol BS9 3EQ
Tel: 0117 950-9621
*Holistic health, happiness and
humour workshops and consultancy.*

Christine Williams
Vine Cottage
156 Manor Road
Fishponds
Bristol BS16 2EN
Tel: 0117 965-0156
Qualified Social Worker,
'Happiness' workshops/individuals/
families/children

Celia Louise
Tel/fax: 01535 637050
www.rowantree.co.uk/info/wow
Reiki master, hypnotherapy, NLP.
Gives talks and workshops
nationwide.

Barry Mapp
The House of Learning
1A Stagborough Way
Stourport-on-Severn
Worcs DY13 8SP
Tel/fax: 01299 877201
Fun, joy and happiness at school
and in the workplace.

Rosie Teanby
15 Kershope Drive
Oakwood
Derby DE21 2TQ
Nursing, healing and humour.

Chai Lifeline Clinic and
   Services
The Laughter Clinic
Horwood House
Harmony Way
London NW4 2BZ
Tel: 0181 202-2211
Fax: 0181 202-2111
Helpline: 0181 202-4567

Carl Munson
The Institute of Joy
30 High Street
Bishops Castle
SY9 5BQ
Tel: 01588 638381
Fax: 01588 638038

EUROPE

The Centre in Favour of Laughter
Dr Dhyan Sutorius
Jupiter 1007
NL-1117 TX Duivendrecht
Netherlands
Tel: (31 20) 6900289

USA

The Option Institute
2080 S Undermountain Road
Sheffield
MA 01257
Tel: 413 229-2100
Fax: 413 229-8931
Email: happiness@option.org
Offers year round programmes
including The Happiness Option
and Happiness Is A Choice.

The Humor Project
c/o Dr Joel Goodman
480 Broadway Ste 210
Saratoga Springs
NY 12866
Tel: 518 587-8770
Fax: 800 600-4242

American Association of
   Therapeutic Humor
222 S Meramec Ste 303

St Louis
MO 63105
Tel: 314 863-6232
Great resource for books, courses,
organizations and events.
Newsletter available.

Carolina Health and Humor
  Association
Ruth Hamilton
5223 Revere Road
Durham
NC 27713
Developed the 'Hospital Humor
Wagon'. Workshops and newsletter.

Gesundheit Institute
Patch Adams, MD
6855 Washington Blvd
Arlington
VA 22213
Tel: 703 525-8169
Fax: 703 532-6132
Dr Adams is a clown, generally
silly person, teacher of silliness and
workshop lecturer on humour and
laughter meditation.

Karyn Buxman
Humorx
PO Box 1273
Hannibal
MO 63401
Tel: 1-800-8-HUMORX
  (800-848-6679)
  573 221-9086
Fax: 573 221-7226
Email: karyn@humorx.com

Leslie Gibson RN, BS
Morton Plant Mease Health Care

323 Jeffords Street #16
Clearwater
FL 34617-0210
24hr tel: 813 462-7841
Fax: 813 733-9167
Humor and laughter workshops,
taining, author of Laughter: The
Universal Language.

Donna Strickland
PO Box 18423
Denver
CO 80218
Tel: 303 777-7997
Laughter, Humor and Play
Workshops, Teambuilding.

Annette Goodheart
635 N Alisos Street
Santa Barbara
CA 03103
Tel: 805 966-0025
Fax: 805 966-6146

Patty Wooten, RN
PO Box 8484
Santa Cruz
CA 95061-8484
Tel: 408 460-1600
Fax: 408 460-1601

AUSTRALIA

Helen Grover
Laughter Workshops
PO Box 575
Coogee
NSW 2034

BOOKS AND CASSETTES

P. Adams, *Good Health is a Laughing Matter* (Better Life Books, 1992).

Janice Anderson, *History of Movie Comedy* (Hamlyn, 1985).

M. Argyle, *The Psychology of Happiness* (Methuen, 1987).

B. Basso and J. Klosek, *This Job Should Be Fun* (Bob Adams Inc., 1991).

B. Bokun, *Humour Therapy* (Vita Books, 1986).

E. de Bono, *The Happiness Purpose* (Penguin, 1977).

N. Cousins, *Anatomy of an Illness* (New York: Norton, 1979). Videotape also available from the publishers.

——, *Head First: The Biology of Hope.*

——, *The Healing Heart.*

D. Einon, *Creative Play* (Penguin, 1986).

G.C. Ellenbogen, *The Directory of Humor Magazines and Humor Organizations in America and Canada* (New York: Wry-Bred Press, Inc., 1985).

Dr. A. Ellis, *Fun as Psychotherapy* (cassette tape, available from Institute for Rational-Emotive Therapy: 45 East 65th Street, New York, NY 10021-6593).

Dr. A. Ellis and Dr. I. Becker, *A Guide to Personal Happiness* (Wilshire, 1982).

Foundation for Inner Peace, *A Course in Miracles* (Arkana, 1985).

S. Freud, *Jokes and their Relation to the Unconscious* (New York: Norton, 1928; 1960).

W.F. Fry, Jr and M. Allan, *Make 'Em Laugh* (Palo Alto, CA: Science and Behavior Books, 1975).

R. Fulgham, *All I Really Need to Know I Learned in Kindergarten* (Ballantine, 1989).

L. Gibson, *Creating a Humor Program: Facilitator's Guide and Videotape* (available from Morton Plant Mease Health Care: 323 Jeffords Street #16, Clearwater FL 34617).

L. Gibson, *Laughter, the Universal Language* (New York: Pegasus Expressions, 1990).

M. de Gruyter, *International Journal of Humor Research* (available from 200 Saw Mill River Road, Hawthorne, NY 10532).

Happiness Project, The, *The Laughter Album – 30 mins of pure laughter* (cassette).

L. Hodgkinson, *Smile Therapy* (MacDonald Optima, 1987).

M. Holden, *Relationships & Enlightenment* (available from: Elms Court, Oxford OX2 9LP).

——, *Accepting Joy & Being Good Enough* (cassette).

R. Holden, *Stress Busters* (Thorsons, 1992).

——, *Living Wonderfully* (Thorsons, 1994).

——, *How To Be Happy* (QED Documentary, BBC Education booklet. Video also available).

——, *Happiness Now* (Hodder & Stoughton, 1998).

——, *The Inner Smile Meditation* (cassette tape).

Dr. G. Jampolsky, *Love is Letting go of Fear* (Berkeley, CA: Celestial Arts, 1979).

'Children as Teachers of Peace', Joyce and Barry Vissell (eds), in *Models of Love: The Parent-Child Journey* (Ramira Publishing, 1986).

W.E. Kelly, *Laughter and Learning* (J. Weston Walch, 1988).

B.A. Kipfer, *14,000 Things To Be Happy About* (Workman, 1990).

M.L. Kushner, *The Light Touch* (Simon & Schuster, 1990).

D. LeFevre, *New Games for the Whole Family* (Perigree Books, 1988).

M. Masheder, *Let's Play Together* (Green Print, 1989).

A. Matthews, *Being Happy* (Media Masters Pte Ltd, 1988).

R. Moody, *Laugh After Laugh: The Healing Power of Humor* (The Humor Project: 480 Broadway Ste 210, Saratoga Springs, NY 12866).

D. Myers, *The Pursuit of Happiness* (Avon Books, 1992).

The New Games Book (available from New Games Foundation: PO Box 7901, San Francisco, CA 94120).

V. Peale (ed.), *Joy and Enthusiasm* (Cedar, 1990).

B. Renshaw, *Relaxation for Happiness* (cassette).

M.D. Roland, *Absolute Happiness* (Hay House, 1995).

Masami Saionji, *The Golden Key to Happiness* (Element Books, 1995).

B. Siegel, *Humour and Healing* (cassette).

J.J. Sloan, *A Pocket Guide to a Happy Life* (Agape House, 1998).

C. & L. Spezzano, *Happiness Is The Best Revenge* (Vision Products Ltd, 1997).

——, *The Irresistable You* (cassette tape available from Creative Leadership: Townsend, Poulshot, Devizes SN10 1SD).

M. Weinstein and J. Goodman, *Playfair* (Impact, 1980).

D. Welliver, *Laughing Together* (Brethren Press, 1986).

The Whole Mirth Catalogue (available from 1034 Page Street, San Francisco, CA 94117). Catalogue of books and toys.

M. Williamson, *Return to Love* (HarperCollins, 1992).

——, *Happiness Is a Decision* (cassette).

——, *Joy – Becoming Your Potential* (cassette).

Z. Ziglar, *Top Performance* (Berkeley Books, 1986).

STRESS BUSTERS

Learn to relieve stress and achieve positive health, peak performance and personal happiness.

Stress Busters is a creative, practical guide to successful stress control – packed with effective strategies for relieving, releasing and controlling stress. There are over 101 tips, tactics and techniques, including yoga, aromatherapy, massage, meditation and diet, all designed to help you find:

- Inner calm
- Deep relaxation
- Greater confidence
- Sounder sleep
- Pain relief
- Better health
- Happy relationships
- More energy

STOP THINKING, START LIVING

'Happy people understand, either instinctively or because they have been taught, that the name of the game is to enjoy life rather than think about it. If you are constantly analysing or keeping score of your life, you will always be able to find fault in whatever you are doing.'

Revolutionary in its simplicity and accessible to all, *Stop Thinking, Start Living* offers profound short-term, common-sense methods that allow you to let go of negativity and tap into your natural state of wellbeing.

In this indispensable handbook, Richard Carlson demonstrates how we can change everything in our lives – earn more money, meet new friends, get a new job – yet still feel dissatisfied. Happiness, he says, is not 'out there' but within, a state of mind that is independent of circumstance: 'If you begin to see that your thoughts are not the real thing – they're just thoughts and as thoughts they can't hurt you – your entire life will begin to change *today*.'

Carlson's step-by-step guide explains:

- how your thoughts determine how you feel
- why thinking about problems only makes them worse
- that thoughts come and go – you are free to choose at any moment which to hold on to and which to let go of
- straightforward methods for conquering depression
- how to dismiss negative thoughts and discover inner peace
- how to overcome lifelong pessimism and start really living

Richard Carlson PhD is a stress consultant in private practice and the bestselling author of seven books, including *Don't Sweat the Small Stuff* and *Slowing Down to the Speed of Life*. He is also the co-author of *Handbook for the Soul*.

EMOTIONAL CONFIDENCE

Do you ever feel that your emotions run away with you? Perhaps you suspect that your behaviour is affected by old emotional hurts which need help to heal. In this practical and sympathetic book, Gael Lindenfield helps you to manage your emotions so that you can create more balance and success in both your working life and your personal life.

Emotional Confidence helps you to:

- Soothe your sensitivity
- Control runaway feelings
- feel more assertive and positive

With a seven-step emotional healing strategy, techniques to help you lift your spirits, build confidence and gain control, you will find Gael Lindenfield's advice invaluable.

Gael Lindenfield is the author of the bestselling *Self Motivation* (book and audio), *The Positive Woman*, *Super Confidence*, *Self Esteem*, *Confident Children*, *Managing Anger* and *Assert Yourself*. She works as a psychotherapist and group work consultant, running successful courses in personal development.